NURTURING AT-RISK YOUTH
IN MATH AND SCIENCE:

Curriculum and Teaching Considerations

Randolf Tobias

National Educational Service

Bloomington, Indiana 1992

recycled paper

Cover design by Brian Thatcher

Printed in the United States of America

ISBN 1-879639-20-3

Dedication

To Ruth, the sole survivor of my immediate family—a family whose nurturing was essential to my very being.

—Randolf Tobias

Acknowledgements

I would like to express my sincere thanks to Eleanor Armour-Thomas, not only for her contributing chapter, but for her editorial work on portions of this manuscript; thanks also go to Howard Margolis, for sharing relevant resources on the educationally at risk and reminding me that "reading within mathematics" is also crucial to the work. Thank you, Sheila Hollander, for the warm dialogue and sharing the results of your research. Also, to the contributing writers of the text, thank you—there would be no book without you. And last but not least, I would like to acknowledge Nancy Shin and Tom Moone of National Educational Service for their invaluable technical assistance.

—*Randolf Tobias*

About the Contributors

EVERARD BARRETT is an associate professor in the mathematics department of the State University of New York at Westbury, and President of Professor B. Enterprises Inc. The Professor B. endeavor consists of original sets of strategies and techniques designed for the accelerated teaching and learning of mathematics by all children. Barrett's techniques gained national recognition because of high assessment ratings given by school districts located in major American cities. In 1980, Professor Barrett gained international recognition when he was commissioned by the Director of UNESCO to a consultantship at the request of the governments of Granada, Jamaica, and St. Lucia. He has since addressed the United Nations Development Program's "Innovative Approaches to Meeting Basic Learning Needs," a follow-up to a major worldwide educational conference held in Jompien, Thailand, in 1990.

Professor Barrett has worked directly with children and teachers in elementary school classrooms since 1973, and he constantly relies on teacher feedback to rethink and alter his training approaches. He firmly believes that quality pedagogy can only evolve from hard work, commitment, and dedication.

LYNNE K. CONRAD has been an elementary classroom and science teacher and has worked for the New York City Central Board of Education on several panels. A graduate of the specialization and leadership programs offered through the Institute for the Advancement of Mathematics and Science, she is currently acting associate director of the institute.

MADELINE J. LONG is the director of the Institute for the Advancement of Mathematics and Science at Long Island Univesity's Brooklyn campus. It was her dream and vision which enabled the development of THA-MASTER, the nation's first formal retraining program for mathematics and science teachers, from a program which served New York City alone to one which is currently offered in all parts of the United States. Before accepting the position of director of the Institute for the Advancement of Mathematics and Science, she headed the Division of Education at LIU-Brooklyn for fifteen years.

Dr. Long regularly presents papers at professional conferences of the National Council of Teachers of Mathematics, the American Association for the Advancement of Science, and the Association for Supervision and Curriculum Development. She is a member of the New York State Advisory Council on Equity and Excellence in Mathematics and Science; the Mayor's Council on Science and Technology; and the Visiting Committee, Office of Education Programs, Brookhaven National Laboratory. Dr. Long is currently on leave from the institute to serve as program director for the National Science Foundation's Presidential Awards for Excellence in Science and Mathematics Teaching Programs.

ELEANOR ARMOUR-THOMAS received her Ed.D. in educational psychology from Teachers College, Columbia University, in 1984. She completed postdoctoral work at Yale University in 1986. From 1986 to 1989 she was a research affiliate in the Department of Psychology at Yale University and currently is an assistant professor of educational psychology in the Department of Secondary Education at Queens College of the City University of New York. Widely published in the field of educational psychology, Dr. Thomas's primary research is in the area of assessment of cognitive and metacognitive competence in ethnic minority populations, particularly those from low socio-economic backgrounds. She is also interested in the implications of this work for pedagogical and curricula interventions.

RANDOLF A. TOBIAS is chairperson of the Graduate Department of Educational and Community Programs at Queens College of the City University of New York. Prior to his present position, he served as associated dean for special programs, Queens College (CUNY); director of the Division of Teacher Education at Winston-Salem State University and Shaw University; and assistant professor of Teacher Education, Long Island University, the Brooklyn campus. As a Mellon Fellow in 1983, Dr. Tobias examined supervisory roles aimed at improving curriculum and teaching within alternative neighborhood schools. He has consulted with school systems and universities on curriculum and teaching approaches for increasing the learning potential of the educationally at risk. As an associate professor within the School Administration and Supervision Program at Queens College, Dr. Tobias is currently involved in the training of prospective principals and assistant principals.

Table of Contents

Introduction

Randolf Tobias

Is the term "at-risk youth" simply a new shine on an old pair of shoes? Are we referring to the traditional disadvantaged; or those from low socioeconomic backgrounds; perhaps exceptional learners; or even oppressed children of color? Are there common denominators that link these children from all walks of life? These and other questions are at the forefront of national and regional conferences. Comer (1987) defines high-risk children as those who underachieve despite intellectual endowment and, as a result, will underachieve as adults. Slavin (1989) states that a student described as at risk is one who is in danger of failing to complete his or her education with an adequate level of skills.

The six common denominators of the educationally at risk appear to be:

1. Academic underachievement;

2. Poor school attendance;

3. Low self esteem;

4. Negative attitudes toward school;

5. Retention in grades for one or more years; and

6. High dropout rates from school.

(For additional discussion of the educationally at risk, see Armour-Thomas's chapter six, "Mathematical Competence and the Educationally At Risk Learner: Implications for Assessment".)

Changes within the social environment that have profound effects upon the human condition have added more dimensions to today's disadvantaged populations. These problems go beyond such labels as underachiever, slow learner, exceptional learner, and the impoverished. At-risk populations are more complex than their counterparts of the sixties and seventies. Our nation's public schools now have to contend with additional problems of young victims—victims of child abuse, substance abuse, suicide, AIDS, homelessness, as well as foster care. These are today's disadvantaged. They come to us with physical, mental, psychological, and emotional scars—from all walks of life, from all socioeconomic backgrounds.

Armour-Thomas (chapter six) states that mathematics and science are the very areas from which the continued growth of the American economy will depend, and from which a high level of cognitive competence will be expected from its workers. This is why this text was written.

Nurturing At-Risk Youth in Math and Science is intended as a curriculum and teacher training accompaniment, which, when applied, can enhance mathematics and science proficiency among at-risk youth. For many of this population who tend to be frightened of these subjects, the text will also suggest curriculum and teaching strategies to raise students' confidence and self-esteem and simultaneously raise their level of mathematics and science interest. The author believes that the process of raising students' confidence and self-esteem in mathematics and science serves to both reduce anxiety and demystify the content area, making these subjects "doable."

In chapter one data covering a period of approximately seven years is presented concerning mathematics and science proficiency of at-risk youth. Sources of these data are generated from the United States Department of Education, National Science Foundation, National Assessment of

Educational Progress, American Association for the Advancement of Science, and the Rand Corporation.

Chapter two discusses the activities of the Institute for the Advancement of Mathematics and Science in the preparation of teachers. Though the institute's major thrust is basically in-service preparation, some discussion is given to pre-service projections of the institute. IAMS's efforts are currently supported by the National Science Foundation, and it is probably the only program of its type in the nation. Dr. Madeleine J. Long, the institute's director, believes that because of the program's positive track record, IAMS could serve as a national prototype for teacher preparation in mathematics and science. Some assessment data of the institute's effort are provided. IAMS's strategies are already in place at a number of universities and school districts across the nation.

Chapter three, "Teaching Mathematics and Science through Context: Unleashing the Power of the Contextual Learner," is both a provocative and exciting proposition. Twenty-two years went into developing and testing Everard Barrett's unique teaching strategy, which has gained national acclaim in cities such as Chicago, Boston, Newark, New York, Dallas, and Atlanta. In chapter four, "Other Programs and Strategies," positive and concrete results for at-risk youth are explored. The Science Skills Center, the Computer Assisted Learning Center, and the Institute for Independent Education are highlighted. There is also discussion of the effective roles of parent intervention strategies and effective communication arts as vehicles to increase math and science proficiency among all youth.

Too many low-income children believe that high achievement in mathematics and science is an impossible dream. They perceive these subjects as "too hard" and believe very early in their educational experience that they are just not smart enough. Low expectations on the part of teachers, coupled with an already established student fear of math and science, make achievement improbable.

Chapter five will explore possible ways of raising student self-confidence and self-esteem through creative math and science teaching. A creative teaching discussion will hopefully engage the reader to consider such themes as math and science demystification; the relationship of math and science to student experiences; teaching math and science from an interdisciplinary perspective; ethnocentric approaches; and practical applications.

Eleanor Armour-Thomas begins chapter six with an examination of the concept of the educationally at-risk learner. Next, the National Council of Teachers of Mathematics standards are set forth to delineate the mathematical competencies expected of the at-risk learner. A review of the extant knowledge base follows with respect to factors influencing mathematical performance, with consideration given to how such information might be used to better understand the areas of strengths and weaknesses of the at-risk learner. The implications of this knowledge base for assessment is then explored. Finally, recommendations for educational policymakers and classroom teachers with respect to assessment issues are given.

Nurturing At-Risk Youth in Math and Science attempts to convey to school administrators, supervisors, teachers, and teacher educators that we can all make a difference in the lives of these youngsters. This difference is demonstrated in the text through the presentation of positive creative programs that are presently in existence. (See chapter four, "Other Programs and Strategies That Work in Teaching Mathematics and Science to At-Risk Youth," for assessment data.)

As the nation attempts to restructure its schools, there is a belief that this process is a must in order to prepare children (particularly at-risk youth) for the twenty-first century. Schools and teacher education programs, however, are not enough to save children. A team effort of colleges, schools, parents, industry, and community residents working together can eventually bring at-risk youth well within the realm of safety.

The discussion put forward in this text is not for the purpose of handling the actual subject-content of mathematics and science. A many-volumed library would be needed to accomplish this task. This volume, however, represents a sharing of ideas for the consideration of how to nurture at-risk youth in subject areas in which they have been traditionally afraid.

There are purposeful messages within these pages: some of the messages are apparent, some not so apparent. The first message is to tell and convince at-risk youth that they can learn mathematics and science, and that these fields are not difficult to master. Second, we as teachers and teacher trainers must provide the professional skills and strategies for nurturing and, in cooperation with families and the community at large, enable youngsters to academically achieve. Third, today's disadvantaged youngsters must be able to compete successfully in mathematics, science, and technology, in order to become adults that have the advantage in tomorrow's super-technological world. Last but not least, enabling at-risk youth to achieve in these areas is actually an investment in America's future. America needs more mathematicians and scientists if it is to compete successfully with its foreign neighbors. Recent findings of the Rand Corporation, the American Association for the Advancement of Science, and the National Assessment of Educational Progress indicate that America is not competing that well within the math and science arenas.

In addition, to the short-range teaching strategies put forth in this volume, the entire American community must become involved in cooperative long-range planning and activity designed to restructure education for the educational survival of all youth.

References

Comer, James. (1987). "New Haven's School—Community Connection." *Educational Leadership* 44(6):13-16.

Slavin, R. E., and Madden, N. A. (1989). "What Works for Students At Risk: A Research Synthesis." *Educational Leadership* 46(5):4-12.

1. Mathematics and Science Proficiency Among At-Risk Youth: What Is the State of the Art?

Randolf Tobias

The National Science Foundation asked the Rand Corporation to undertake a study of the way the nation's educational system distributes access toward learning mathematics and science among various groups of students (Oakes, 1990). The study, entitled "Multiplying Inequalities: The Effects of Race, Social Class and Tracking on Opportunities to Learn Mathematics and Science" (1990), examined access in five significant areas:

1. The distribution of judgment about ability;

2. Access to science and mathematics programs;

3. Access to qualified teachers;

4. Access to resources; and

5. Access to classroom opportunities.

With respect to "access to science and mathematics programs," the study concluded that

> [w]ith the exception of slightly greater amounts of time allocated to mathematics instruction in elementary schools with high concentration of low-income and minority children, students from groups that as adults consistently achieve and participate less in science and mathematics have less access to science and mathematics curriculum. (vii)

This fact is particularly true for low-income African American and Hispanic students enrolled in secondary schools, where they are the majority and have less extensive and less demanding science and mathematics programs available to them (Oakes, 1990). The study also highlighted that these same populations have fewer opportunities to take critical courses that prepare them for science and mathematics study after geometry in junior high school and algebra and calculus in high school. This inequality of access is often compounded by inequalities in the opportunities available to various groups of students within schools, because of the low-track courses that are usually disproportionately filled with high percentages of low-income and minority students. The findings of Rand in this regard corroborates statements of Dr. Shirley Malcolm (1989) of the American Association for the Advancement of Science:

1. Only one out of five black students take physics within American high schools; and

2. Only 7% of black students major in science within American high schools.

Another interesting Rand finding is that high-ability students at low socioeconomic status (SES) high-minority schools may actually have fewer opportunities than low-ability students who attend more advantaged schools (Oakes, 1990).

The area of "access to qualified teachers" also brought about several important findings. Principals of racially mixed and high-minority schools often complained that lack of teacher interest and inadequate preparation to teach caused serious problems at their schools. In contrast, schools whose students are predominantly economically advantaged and white as well as and suburban schools employ teachers who are, on the average, more qualified (Oakes, 1990). Rand's findings that low-income and minority students have less contact with qualified science and mathematics teachers not only speak of the numbers of these teachers available but also of large differences in certification status and academic and teaching experiences, particularly at the secondary level. Conversely, middle-income and white students have greater access to science and math teachers who are certified to teach their subjects. Educationally at risk students who have been grouped and tracked into low-ability classes within junior and senior high schools are being taught by teachers considerably less qualified than those that are teaching other levels.

The inequities of "access to resources" are similar. Students who attend schools in low socioeconomic areas have unequal access to science and mathematics facilities and equipment, e.g., computers and science laboratories. Even the science and mathematics textbooks are of lower quality.

Though Rand treated the areas of "distribution of judgments about ability" and "access to classroom opportunities" as separate research issues, the relationship between the two is quite profound. Assessments of academic ability of the educationally at risk are primarily made from achievement test scores. These children are then grouped and tracked in low-ability classes. These classes often parallel race and social class differences offering reduced educational opportunities.

A disproportionate percentage of teachers who teach in schools located in low socio-economic areas judge their science and mathematics to have low ability (Oakes, 1990):

> Thus, to the extent that placement in classes at different levels affects students' opportunities to learn and the evidence from our study suggests that the effects are quite profound—minority students disproportionately suffer whatever disadvantages accrue to students in low-track classes. (vii)

Teachers who teach in inner-city schools or teach low-track classes appear to place less emphasis on inquiry and problem-solving skills; promotion of active involvement in mathematics and science learning; and access to engaging classroom experiences and teacher expectations for their out-of-school learning.

Specifically, what is the nature and quality of educational programs available to students who score below the national average on standardized tests in basic skills, as well as for those whom negative judgments have been made regarding their ability by teachers? There are two questions that are particularly relevant to the investigation of precollege mathematics and science experiences of the educationally at-risk learner:

1. What is the nature and quality of mathematics and science curricula that are used for students in low-track classes?

2. What is the nature and quality of mathematics and science instruction implemented in low-track classes?

Curricula Programs in Mathematics and Science

Evidence converging from different sources (e.g., National Longitudinal study, High School and Beyond study, and National Assessment of Educational Progress) point to the importance of participation in high school courses and achievement in mathematics and science (Jones et al., 1986; Welch, Anderson, and Harris, 1982). Furthermore, there is also some evidence that attests to the relationship between the number of courses made available to students and the nature and quality of student learning (e.g., Peng, Owings, and Fetters, 1981; Rock et al., 1985). For example, the National Survey of Science and Mathematics Education (NSSME) findings on schools serving the largest concentration of low-income students shows that middle schools and junior high schools serving the largest concentration of low-income students (schools that most ethnic minorities attend) offered fewer mathematics (roughly 3 classes per 100 students) and science (roughly 2.5 classes per 100 students) programs. Similarly, the High School and Beyond data indicated not only that senior high schools serving low-income students offered fewer advanced placement courses (Ekstrom, Goertz, and Rock, 1988), but that fewer students at such schools enrolled in academically rigorous mathematics and science courses compared to their college-bound colleagues at high-income schools (Rock et al., 1985).

A pattern emerges from these data that indicates a strong relationship between low-income, ethnic minority status and fewer offerings for advanced, college-preparatory courses. Since these characteristics are included in the profile of the educationally-at-risk learner, it is logical to assume that relatively few opportunities are open to them for academically rigorous experiences in mathematics and science.

In general, a consistent finding is that students in low-track classes are not required to take many mathematics and science courses and that few such courses are available to them (Guthrie and Leventhal, 1985; Sanders, Stone, and LaFollette, 1987; Vanfossen, Jones, and Spade, 1985).

Nature and Quality of Curriculum

The nature and quality of curriculum focus provides useful information regarding the kinds of knowledge and skills to which students are exposed for cultivating cognitive competence. Listed below are findings from research that investigated various aspects of curriculum:

- Curriculum in low-track classes focuses on less rigorous topics and low-level skills whereas high-track classes emphasize more rigorous topics and complex thinking skills (Burgess, 1983, 1984; Nystrand and Gamoran, 1988; Oakes, 1985)

- Goals in mathematics and science in low SES schools serving high concentrations of ethnic minority students focus on the relevance of science in daily life and computational skills in mathematics, whereas in high-track classes teachers expect students to develop inquiry and laboratory skills and to utilize a problem-solving approach in content

Nature and Quality of Pedagogy in Mathematics and Science

What kinds of instructional practices, learning experiences, and arrangements are available to the educationally-at-risk learner? Findings parallel those of curricula studies.

In low-track classes instructional strategies focus on recitation, the use of worksheets, and decomposability of information into isolated bits of information (Keddie, 1971; Oakes, 1985; Page, 1987). Students in low-track classes at the junior and senior high school levels are not exposed to opportunities in mathematics and science that would nurture cognitive competence.

Perhaps low performance of at-risk youth in mathematics and science is symptomatic of a more fundamental problem of American educational achievement in these areas. Out of fourteen industrial countries, America ranked twelfth in chemistry and last in biology achievement scores (Malcolm, 1989). According to the Office of Educational Research and Improvement of the United States Department of Education, fewer and fewer American students appear able to learn more difficult math concepts and skills. One of the findings released by the National Assessment of Educational Progress (NAEP) in 1990 is that the average twelfth grader is about to leave high school and enter the work force armed with math skills that go little beyond handling decimals, percents, fractions, and simple algebra (see Table 1) (U.S. Department of Education, 1991):

> About 72 percent of 4th graders in the national sampling of public and private school students accurately answered questions on simple additive reasoning and problem solving with whole numbers. By 8th grade, virtually all could do this basic math and 67 percent showed an understanding of multiplication and division of whole numbers and problems involving more than one step. But only 14 percent could successfully do problems involving fractions, decimals, percents, and simple algebra. All 12th graders could do

addition and subtraction and more than 90 percent could do multiplication and division. But less than half were successful with decimals, fractions, percents, and simple algebra, and only 5 percent showed an understanding of geometry and algebra that suggested they were ready for advanced college mathematics.

Table I

		Grade 4	Grade 8	Grade 12
Average Student Proficiency Nationally		216	265	295
Level Description		Percentage of students at or above this level		
200	Simple additive reasoning and problem solving with whole numbers	72	98	100
250	Simple multiplicative reasoning and two-step problem solving	11	67	91
300	Reasoning and problem solving involving fractions, decimals, percents, elementary geometry, and simple algebra	0	14	46
350	Reasoning and problem solving involving geometry, algebra, and beginning statistics and probability	0	0	

Results of the NAEP national sample

Table reprinted from the OERI Bulletin, Summer 1991, Page 1

Implications

Has anything basically changed since Brown vs. Topeka, Kansas, Board of Education, 1954, or the Coleman Study (Equality of Educational Opportunity), 1966? Both the court decision and the report ten years hence dealt with the inequality of segregated schools for black children. The former examined the devastating effects of a de jure segregated school system, and the latter examined the devastating effects of a de facto segregated school system. Both events dealt with inequality of educational opportunity.

What does educational inequality mean for at-risk youth in the areas of mathematics and science?

- Considerably less access to science and mathematics knowledge at school

- Fewer material resources

- Less engaging learning activities in their classrooms

- Less qualified teachers

Current educational practices within our schools are helping to create and perpetuate differences in achievement and participation in "across the board" educational opportunity. Cummins (1986) points out, for example, that almost a decade after the nondiscriminatory assessment provision of Public Law 94-142, there has been a disproportionate share of Hispanic students in Texas that have been labeled learning disabled. (In New York City there appears to be a disproportionate share of black students labeled educably retarded and emotionally handicapped as compared to white students who are labeled learning disabled.) Low scores on standardized tests created the grouping and tracking syndrome still prevalent in public schools today. Children who are placed in slow groups, and thus homogeneously tracked from grade to grade, receive watered-down subject content (Tobias, 1978). Although the decisions are usually well intentioned, considerable evidence suggests that tracking, especially at secondary schools, fails to increase learning generally and has the unfortunate consequence of widening the achievement gaps between students judged to be more and less able (Oakes, 1990).

The low-level courses available or required of these students, the inadequate quantity and quality of mathematics and science curriculum and instruction to which they are socialized, place them at risk in tomorrow's technological world. It is unlikely, if this trend continues, that they will be equipped with the necessary mathematical and scientific knowledge and skills for life in the twenty-first century. These findings also raise some troubling concerns with regard to the availability and access of educational resources for at-risk youth from low-income backgrounds. It would appear that, despite the nation's verbal commitment to the twin ideals of equity and social justice for all children, educational opportunities still seem to be tied to ethnic, political, and economic status.

It is apparent that solving these problems is not easy. The nature of these problems raises ethical as well as educational issues. There is no doubt that fundamental educational policy on the state level must change to address the vital educational needs of at-risk youth. Historically, fundamental policy changes in education were accomplished through judicial decisions and legislation.

However long judicial or legislative procedures and processes take to rectify institutional errors, these avenues should be pursued. Public Law 94-142 (the Education of All Handicapped Children's Act), for example, literally took years to enact. The wait, however, was worth it, since this legislation (in spite of its state-level procedural bugs) has insisted that all children from ages three to twenty-one, regardless of handicap, receive a free education *that is least restrictive to their intellectual growth.* Superb!

Let us now look at some short-range approaches within the ensuing chapters.

References

Burgess, R. G. (1983). *Experiencing Comprehensive Education: A Study of Bishop McGregor School.* London: Methuen.

---. (1984). "It's Not a Proper Subject: It's Just Newsom." In *Defining the Curriculum,* ed. I. Goodson and S. Ball. London: The Falmer Press.

Cummins, Jim. (1986). "Empowering Minority Students: A Framework for Intervention." *Harvard Educational Review* 56 (1): 28-43.

Ekstrom, R. B., Goertz, M. E., and Rock, D. (1988). *Education and American Youth.* Philadelphia: The Falmer Press.

Guthrie, L. F., and Leventhal, C. (1985). "Opportunities for Scientific Literacy for High School Students." Paper presented at the Annual Meeting of the American Educational Research Association, Chicago.

Jones, L. V., Davenport, E. C., Bryson, Bekhuis, T., and Zwick, R. (1986). "Mathematics and Science Test Scores as Related to Courses Taken in High School and Other Factors," *Journal of Educational Measurement* 23 (3): 197-208.

Keddie, N. (1971). "Classroom Knowledge." In *Knowledge and Control,* ed. M.F.D. Young. London: Collier-MacMillan.

Malcolm, S. (1989). The American Association for the Advancement of Science. A quotation from a public television production entitled "Who Will Do Science?" New York: WNET, TV, Channel 13.

Nystrand, M., and Gamoran, A. (1988). *A Study of Instruction as Discourse.* Madison: Wisconsin Center for Education Research.

Oakes, J. (1985). *Keeping Track: How Schools Structure Inequality.* New Haven: Yale University Press.

---. (1990). *Multiplying Inequalities: The Effects of Race, Social Class and Tracking on Opportunities to Learn Mathematics and Science.* Santa Monica: The Rand Corporation, v-xiii.

Page, R. (1987). "Lower-Track Classes at a College-Preparatory School: A Caricature of Educational Encounters." In *Interpretive Ethnography of Education: At Home and Abroad,* ed. G. Spindler and L. Spindler. Hillsdale: Erlbaum.

Peng, S. S., Owings, J. A., and Fetters, W. B. (1981). "Effective High Schools: What Are Their Attributes?" Paper presented at the Annual Meeting of the American Statistical Association, Cincinnati, Ohio.

Rock, D., Braun, H. I., and Rosenbaum, P. R. (1985). *Excellence in High School Education: Cross-sectional Study, 1980-1982.* Final Report. Princeton: Educational Testing Service.

Sanders, N., Stone, N., and LaFollette, J. (1987). *The California Curriculum Study: Paths Through High School.* Sacramento: California State Department of Education.

Tobias, R. (1978). "Education-Reading and Testing." In *Human Issues and Human Values,* ed. Randolf Tobias. Raleigh: Davis and Foy Publishers for Council of Concerned African American Christians, 29.

United States Department of Education. (Summer, 1991). Office of Educational Research and Improvement (OERI) Bulletin, 1-2.

Vanfossen, B. E., Jones, J. D., and Spade, J. Z. (1985). "Curriculum Tracking: Courses and Consequences." Paper presented at the Annual Meeting of the American Educational Research Association, Chicago.

Welch, W. W., Anderson, R. E., and Harris, L. J. (1982). "The Effects of Schooling on Mathematics Achievement." *American Educational Research Journal*: 19, 143-145.

2. "You're Teaching Mathematics!" In-service and Pre-service Teacher Preparation in Mathematics and Science

Madeleine J. Long and Lynne K. Conrad

Dr. Genevieve Knight, professor of mathematics at Coppin State College and member of the Executive Board of the Mathematical Association of America's Task Force on Minorities in America, is herself a minority teacher. Fortunate enough to have grown up in a family that placed a high value on education, she is concerned about today's students in general and at-risk students in particular, especially about the quality of the education they receive in mathematics. In an address to a group of New York City teachers about teaching mathematics to at-risk students, Dr. Knight concluded by stating:

> Mathematics is power. When a child begins to gain control of numbers, he begins to gain control of his life. When you walk into a classroom the thing to consider is not that you're teaching at-risk students, but that you're teaching *mathematics*.

Her often repeated point emphasizes the fact that all students require—and deserve—excellent teaching if they are to learn mathematics. Improving teaching for *all* children will necessarily benefit those who most need it—the at-risk students. Dr. Melvin Webb, director of an NSF-funded Comprehensive Resource Center for Minorities at Clark-Atlanta University, often tells audiences that he can determine the number of minority students in a given school by counting the number of "funny math" courses offered and multiplying by 35. His point is clear: simplifying or, as some would say, "watering down" the curriculum works for no one, least of all minority students.

The position taken by Dr. Knight and Dr. Webb is simple: minority students should be given the opportunity to learn the same rigorous content—with the same expectation for success—as other students. They should, in short, be provided with teachers with strong mathematics backgrounds, an awareness of current recommendations on effective teaching strategies, the ability to impart an excitement for the subject, and the skills to engage students in meaningful, *successful* mathematical discoveries.

To achieve maximum impact, at-risk students should be provided, more frequently than they currently are, with teachers of their own ethnic background who understand their problems and can serve as role models. A recent report by the National Research Council points out that

> during the next decade, 30 percent of public school children, but only 5 percent of their mathematics teachers, will be minorities. The inescapable fact is that two demographic forces—increasing black and Hispanic youth in the classrooms, decreasing black and Hispanic graduates in mathematics—will virtually eliminate classroom role models for those students who most need motivation, incentive, and high-quality teaching of mathematics. The underrepresentation of this generation of minorities leads to further underrepresentation in the next, yielding an unending cycle of mathematical poverty. (NRC, 1989)

Where will all these teachers come from? What skills will they need to stem the tide of innumeracy and help today's at-risk youth become tomorrow's success stories? Most important, how will they acquire these skills?

In the past four years, several prestigious organizations have made recommendations concerning the effective training of mathematics teachers. While focusing on slightly different areas, the National Research Council (NRC), the American Association for the Advancement of Science (AAAS), the Mathematical Association of America (MAA), and the National Council of Teachers of Mathematics (NCTM) agree on several basic guidelines for this training.

- Teachers must be taught in a manner similar to how they are to teach—by exploring, conjecturing, communicating, reasoning and so forth...All teachers need an understanding of both the historical development and current applications of mathematics. (NCTM *Standards*, 1989)

- Teachers need to learn contemporary mathematics....in a style consistent with the way in which they will be expected to teach....They need to learn science....so they can teach mathematics in the context where it arises most naturally....And they need to learn the history of mathematics and its impact on society....They themselves need experience in doing mathematics—in exploring, guessing, testing, estimating, arguing and proving. (NRC, 1989)

- From the earliest grade levels, it will be essential that teachers know about developmental psychology and learning theories, and that they have a deep knowledge of mathematics in its interaction with real-world phenomena. (AAAS, 1989)

Such recommendations are addressed primarily to colleges and universities who train future teachers. But what about the thousands of existing elementary and middle school teachers who are faced with the task of walking into the classroom every day and teaching subjects for which few are prepared and of which so many are afraid? What can be done for the out-of-license middle or junior high school teacher who has the responsibility for teaching mathematics or science without the appropriate preparation? Or the elementary teacher with fifteen years of experience who still approaches mathematics and science with trepidation? How does one prevent teachers from passing on such attitudes to students, thus creating a new generation of math-anxious people? How does one break this cycle and render existing teachers sufficiently comfortable with mathematics and science to infect their students with the joy of discovery rather than the fear of failure? And how does one ensure that an increasing number of those teachers will be from groups presently underrepresented?

School districts across the country have attempted to solve these problems for years. Many bring in outside "experts" to run one-shot workshops. Others utilize the services of professional trainers from the publishers of mathematics or science textbooks and materials to demonstrate the most effective use of their products. Still others encourage or require their teachers to attend institutes for more intensive training. Unfortunately, once the workshops, demonstrations, and institutes are over, many participants find themselves back in the classroom with the door closed and no one to turn to for advice and support when they most need it, and the question remains: How can one educate existing teachers, attract more minorities to mathematics and science, change attitudes, and have an impact upon the atmosphere of entire schools?

In one guise or another, the Institute for the Advancement of Mathematics and Science has been responding to this question since 1976. Based in New York City at Long Island University's Brooklyn campus, it has been supported by funds from the National Science Foundation (NSF) and the Fund for the Improvement of Postsecondary Education (FIPSE). It has grown from an informal consortium of educators in the mid-'70s through its formalization as a university institute in 1983 to its present position as developer and disseminator of model in-service teacher training programs for the '90s. Since 1976, the institute's director has designed and implemented a number of in-service programs which have been replicated and adapted by colleges, universities, and school systems and have been responsible for the effective training of mathematics teachers across the country. Three of these programs will be examined in the ensuing pages.

General Institute Philosophy

Each of the institute's programs was designed to meet a specific need, with one being developed before the institute became an "official body." All were funded by NSF and/or FIPSE and provided graduate credit at no cost or reduced tuition with two providing daily stipends for summer study. In spite of different foci, they shared common goals based on tenets which the director felt to be essential for the success of *any* in-service training programs, especially for those dealing with mathematics.

Content Study

Teachers must know considerably more than they will ever be called upon to teach. They must gain a proper perspective of the entire range of mathematics and develop a clear understanding of where their particular level or area fits in the overall pattern, how it is affected by what is taught before, and how, in turn, it affects what is taught afterward. Therefore, the content for the program must be planned as a whole and discussed and digested over an extended period of time. It cannot and should not be a mere selection of discrete, traditional courses, *nor can it be done by any one person.* Among those who must be involved are: department chairs (or the equivalent) from middle schools and junior and senior high schools; teachers from all levels, K-12; scientists and mathematicians; university faculty; and mathematics and science supervisors at the local and state levels. In addition, curriculum guides published by local and state educational agencies and by the National Council of Teachers of Mathematics and the National Science Teachers Association must be consulted.

The first institute program was planned to take account of a 24 credit New York State certification requirement which includes 6 credits in calculus. Others were guided by requirements for K-6 and K-9 certification. The introduction of physical science in one program, requirements of other states, and different local needs necessitated adjustments, all of which were planned with collaborative care. It is not the task of such programs merely to duplicate existing courses offered to mathematics majors; nor is it sufficient to provide watered-down "education-math" courses. It is necessary, rather, to structure both the content and the sequence of the courses to provide current and future *teachers* of the subject with a background of depth and breadth and to give them the sufficient support they need to master the material.

Refresher Courses and Content Workshops

If many of the participants have not studied mathematics or science for years, they may require a course designed to reintroduce them to modes of thinking in the discipline, to review key topics, and to provide material for self-study before the beginning of the actual program. During the program, workshops which include preparation for and review of the course material, problem-solving, attention to topics not part of the formal course, enrichment material and remedial work, and methods and strategies should be conducted by carefully chosen instructors in cooperation with university faculty. Students should be placed in them in accordance with their individual needs as demonstrated during the refresher courses, a pre-test, and, later, progress in the class sessions. The selection of workshop staff is particularly critical here, as adjustments in content and teaching style must be made constantly.

Content Delivery and Staff Selection

More important in some respects than the content itself is the way in which it is delivered. If, as the NCTM'S *Standards* recommend, mathematics should be learned in a process-oriented, problem-solving, group-discovery style, and should be explored through applications in all areas of the curriculum and of the student's world beyond the classroom, then *teachers themselves must be taught mathematics in this way.* Selection of an effective instructional staff thus becomes one of the most critical factors in the program.

Staff should complement each other's skills and have content expertise, enthusiasm for the subject, knowledge of child and adolescent development, familiarity with how school systems work, open attitudes about change, the facility to *model* effective methods rather than "teach" them, the ability to work well with others, and a commitment to the philosophy of the program. Obviously the choice of staff will be based upon the "best fit" possible between the skills needed and the personnel available, but every effort should be made to avoid those who wish to continue doing "business as usual."

Participant Selection

Content-intensive programs require commitment of time and energy—both physical and mental. Those involved in selecting participants must consider a variety of factors that cannot be measured by test scores or pen-and-paper surveys. In addition to aspects of the candidates themselves, it is also important to determine the extent of district and school support for both the program in general and the candidate in particular. A multilevel selection process is therefore considered most effective.

The process must originate in the districts, where interested candidates submit application forms and educational and professional histories. From these submissions, the district ranks the candidates and forwards their applications to the institute office with signed letters of recommendation and support. (Without these letters of support, no candidate can be accepted.)

Perhaps the most essential part of the process is a personal interview of every candidate. These interviews allow the staff to determine enthusiasm, professionalism, and the ability to communicate ideas and work effectively with others. They should be supplemented by both classroom observations and videotapes of candidates teaching mathematics, and, in some cases, by performance on Shulman-type activities. Acceptance must be based not on any one criterion but on the total picture created by all the selection components.

Minority Recruitment

It is generally accepted that for mathematics and science training programs to have maximum impact on the students most at risk, it is necessary to reach as many minority teachers as possible. However, traditional recruitment techniques seem to have had little effect on teachers whose own mathematics and science backgrounds have been determined by the same system which now causes their students to be at risk.

Minority teachers must be carefully recruited by administrators and peers who recognize their potential and support their efforts. They must be encouraged to take risks inherent in any new undertaking and to be assured that a cooperative effort from everyone involved will lead to the success of *all* participants. They need to understand that their contributions to any program are as important to their colleagues as the benefits of the program are to themselves. They must understand that they, by virtue of their past experiences, can become valuable resources for colleagues who require insight into the things that affect their students' success with mathematics and science.

Systemic Cooperation

Programs such as these cannot work if they are imposed by one group upon another; nor can they succeed unless there is respect and cooperation among those who have to work together most closely. Education faculty, mathematics and science faculty, and school personnel must all respect the other's contributions and roles. Precollege educators (teachers, mathematics and science coordinators, principals, and superintendents) and the local and state supervisors of mathematics and science *must* all be involved at every stage of development. *A cooperative network cannot be taken for granted—it must be built and maintained throughout the life of the program.*

All parties must recognize the need for the program, be involved in establishing its goals and objectives, and understand what it takes to implement them. They must be prepared to make commitments, devote the time, and take the risks involved in fulfilling them. They must be willing to see around corners! Trust and understanding must exist between school people and university faculty. Universities must be prepared to give both academically and fiscally; they must be willing to see federal dollars as "venture capital" which permits them to initiate a program to which they must contribute and, ultimately, sustain. Academic departments within universities must have had experience training teachers and must demonstrate an appreciation of the idea that the curriculum sometimes should be differentiated if it is to best serve both teachers of a subject and future researchers.

Finally, there must be a pool of teachers available who can benefit from such a program and who are willing to make the investment its success requires. In short, there must be teachers who are willing to work long hours, engage in rigorous study, work with often recalcitrant colleagues, break established lines of authority and literally chart new paths even when everything in them cries out to stay put and stay safe.

Long-term Study and Support

The kind of in-depth knowledge needed by effective mathematics teachers cannot be acquired in "quick fix" workshops or two-week summer "institutes" which provide the participants with an assortment of clever tricks and send them back to their classrooms with no one to turn to for guidance when things don't go *quite* as anticipated. Effective programs must, of necessity, span a considerable amount of time during which new knowledge can be fully internalized. They must also provide reinforcement to participants in their schools during the school year.

Of equal importance is the development among participants of a network of instructors, staff, and fellow students who can be called on for advice and assistance. A collegial atmosphere in which all participants feel as comfortable about *asking* for help as they do about giving it and in which the staff are looked upon as guides and mentors rather than observers and evaluators is essential.

Adaptability

For a program to have widespread effect, its essential components must be readily adaptable to fit a variety of educational, socioeconomic, and political situations. Since 1976, the institute's programs and their components have been adapted by universities and school systems across the country, and one has been considered as part of a "package" to upgrade mathematics education in parts of Australia.

Program I—Teacher Recertification: Secondary School Mathematics and Science

Supported by funds from the NSF (and later by FIPSE) this program was designed to retrain experienced teachers of other subjects or levels who were in danger of being excessed, to teach mathematics in secondary schools, and to help reduce the teacher shortage in mathematics. It was later expanded to include physics. Although primarily developed to meet the specific needs of recertification in New York City, the prescribed course of study was appropriate for prospective mathematics or science teachers in other locales and has been offered in institutions across the country. Among the program objectives were:

- To cope with the critical and pervasive shortage of mathematics teachers by enabling laid off teachers or those in danger of being laid off to qualify for recertification and appointment as teachers of mathematics

- To present a comprehensive, in-depth study of the most important topics taught in secondary school

- To help teachers understand how students learn mathematics and to comprehend relationships between cognition and the structure and content of today's mathematics curriculum

- To develop skill in the presentation of mathematics to students

Content was selected by choosing from among courses traditionally offered to formal mathematics majors those most relevant to the teaching of secondary school mathematics. The curriculum was designed cooperatively over a one-and-a-half year period and constantly refined during the next four years by mathematicians (including Morris Kline), teachers, and educators. Care was taken to avoid the recreation of existing courses perfectly appropriate for mathematics majors who have three or four years to learn their "trade" but inappropriate and inefficient for the mature, experienced teacher who must do the learning in a year's time. The aim was to develop a kernel of mathematical learning around which graduates would continue to build throughout their career.

The program began with a one-week summer refresher course designed to prepare for the academic year. It introduced mathematical thinking and reviewed essential topics from elementary algebra, geometry, and trigonometry. In a sense it was a "warm-up" for teachers who had not studied formal mathematics in many years and provided them with background for self-study. The academic year program involved four mathematics courses with concomitant workshops and a course in teaching mathematics. Content study commenced with the essentials of mathematics and carried students through the calculus before proceeding further.

Content Study

Classes were held after school four hours (double the usual number) one day per week with four-hour workshops on another day. Rather than following the traditional semester, students took one course at a time during each of five eight-week periods. This sequential organization was a response to the building-block structure of mathematics and enabled participants to satisfy prerequisite requirements and master one subject area before proceeding to the next.

The courses included Survey of Mathematics, Applied Calculus I and II, and an Introduction to Modern Mathematics. The latter was a capstone course which served to guide teachers of mathematics into the world of sophisticated and advanced mathematics through study of Courant and Robins, *What Is Mathematics?*.

The final course, Teaching Mathematics in Secondary Schools, was given in June, after the other courses were completed. Since the participants were experienced teachers, emphasis here was on the pedagogical techniques most relevant to the teaching of secondary school mathematics: verbal problems, heuristics, applications, a critical review of newly developed mathematics curriculum, and the role of the computer in the teaching of mathematics.

Workshops accompanied each course and included individual tutorials, discussion groups, problem-solving sessions, and laboratories conducted concurrently for an additional four hours per week. Students were placed in the workshops in accordance with individual needs as demonstrated during the brief summer refresher course and in class sessions. No group remained static since performance levels generally changed as participants dealt with different content areas. Those who mastered work more quickly than others were provided with opportunities to investigate areas in greater breadth and depth. Included in the workshop sessions were topics which examined the role of computers in education, strategies for teaching mathematics and/or science, and mathematics and science applications in other fields. Here, as well as in the methods course, participants are asked to present and evaluate simulated lessons and use selected teaching materials. The workshop format allowed for dealing effectively with the extreme diversity inevitable among a student population accepted into such a program.

Although the program began with the major focus on mathematics, physics and chemistry programs were added later, designed in the same structural format as the mathematics program: summer refresher, four eight-week content courses with concomitant workshops and laboratories, and a methods course.

Minority Representation

The program was offered on a yearly basis, from 1976 to 1986, to over 300 teachers in New York City. Although the figure varied from year to year, the average minority representation was 25 percent. As more than 70 percent of the program graduates became certified and assumed positions teaching high school mathematics or physics, a significant number of minority teachers returned to the classroom as mentors and role models for their students.

Program II—Mathematics and Science Specialization: Elementary and Middle School

A second program, designed to create expertise in teaching mathematics and science at the elementary and middle school levels, responded to the need to improve instructional competence by introducing teachers to content and was requested by several New York City school superintendents.

Studies done in the early '80s highlighted the need for more effective mathematics and science teaching at this level. The National Science Board attributed lack of ability and interest among children to elementary and middle school teachers with little or no training in these areas. Its report claimed that future teachers pass through the elementary schools learning to detest mathematics and return to teach a new generation to detest it (NSB, 1982). Adequately trained elementary teachers were pivotal in reversing this cycle, but the majority did not have significant college mathematics or science or appropriate methods of teaching them. It was critical, therefore, to locate and train teachers to be competent in mathematics and science at the elementary level. What did not get taught at this level, where attitudes were formed and foundations were constructed for later learning, was difficult to make up later.

An additional problem arose from the failure of women and minorities to do well in mathematics and science coupled with the fact that most elementary teachers were women. In urban areas, many of those women came from minority groups, thus compounding the problem. A key factor to increasing minority representation in mathematics and science seemed to be the creation of successful role models who approached mathematics and science with enthusiasm and high expectations for their students.

In 1982, meetings were held with constituents to discuss elements of a program which could provide in-service mathematics and science training for teachers in grades four to six, those grades critical for first exposure to more formal study.

Program Goals

The aim of the specialization program was to enhance the mathematics and science background of elementary and middle school teachers and to enable them to do limited staff development as part of their teaching responsibilities. Principals were required to provide staff development time for the teachers commencing in the project's second year.

The goals of the program included:

- Developing an in-depth study of selected topics in mathematics, science, and computer science

- Integrating the three disciplines

- Developing curriculum materials

- Increasing teacher's awareness of how mathematics and science help people solve real problems

- Attracting women and other minorities to teaching careers in mathematics and science

- Enabling teachers to deal more effectively with exceptional children, minority children, and women

- Breaking the chain that perpetuates the transfer from teacher to pupil of anxiety and fear regarding mathematics and science.

Program in Practice

The program encompassed two academic years and an intervening summer. The first year and the summer session were devoted to content study and professional development and the second year to leadership training and work with staff development. Because of the amount of academic work required, districts were asked to release participants two half-days a week for a year to attend courses in mathematics and science. (This amounted to the equivalent of thirty to thirty-six full teaching days for each participant and was funded by the districts.) Each day's session consisted of a two-hour class followed by a two-hour science laboratory or mathematics workshop, each of which was offered at two levels, enrichment and review. The structure of the sessions was flexible to allow for continuous self-selection of level by participants as they studied topics with which they were more—or less—comfortable.

Course content began with topics covered in the 4-6 curriculum, then went beyond in the belief that competent teachers must know far more than they would be called upon to teach. The mathematics course covered two semesters of work and included study of the real number system; number theory; algebra; geometries; and probability and statistics. The science course was offered in three ten-week segments covering topics in physics, biology, and geology. Both courses stressed applications to real-world situations and used problem solving to develop many topics.

The summer session included two weeks devoted to a course which introduced participants to the computer and its various uses, allowed them to become familiar with mathematics and science software, and required them to evaluate the computer's effectiveness as an instructional tool in the mathematics or science classroom. The remainder of the summer session provided time for special workshops on topics like manipulatives and metrics, leadership training, lectures on current issues in mathematics and science given by practicing mathematicians and scientists, and development of interdisciplinary approaches to teaching mathematics and science.

The second academic year was designed to provide opportunities for the participants to do limited staff development and to design/refine curriculum. University sessions were reduced to one four-hour *after*-school session per week devoted to peer teaching and curriculum development. Each participant was required to do at least 30 hours of staff development and to produce a viable curriculum project that would be used in his or her school.

Minority Representation

The program was offered to 105 participants at three different sites in the New York metropolitan area. Thirty-four percent of the participants were minority teachers and more than half taught in schools where the minority student population exceeded 75%. The fact that many of these participants were from minority groups was an important first step in providing their minority students with positive role models who reflected not only the personal success they achieved through content mastery but the professional respect such success earned for them.

Program III—Leadership: Elementary and Middle School Mathematics

The specialization program created classroom teachers with expertise in mathematics and science and some limited opportunity to work with colleagues. The success of this program, coupled with recommendations by the Holmes Group and the Carnegie Task Force calling for elementary school specialists, led to the development of a third program designed to create a cadre of elementary and middle school mathematics lead teachers with the ability and authority to effect schoolwide change.

The institute director, responding to requests from superintendents who wanted more teachers trained as specialists, arranged a series of meetings with superintendents, mathematics coordinators, university faculty, participants of past programs, and local and state education department representatives. Under her guidance they planned an intensive content-based program which addressed the needs expressed by the Conference Board of Mathematical Sciences:

> At this level [middle school], mathematics should be taught by people who have special training in this subject....Unfortunately, at the present time there is a severe shortage of qualified mathematics teachers for such positions. Thus renewal is especially critical." (CBMS, 1984)

The director felt that a useful response to the shortage of qualified upper-elementary and middle school mathematics teachers was the development and training of mathematics specialists and resource teams within each school building. Such an approach would be an expedient, appropriate, and cost-effective one for many school districts and teachers.

School districts, individual schools, and a university would form a tightly knit partnership focused on creating mathematics expertise and sophistication for individual school buildings. The most important ingredient, the program participant, would resemble Carnegie's lead teacher, or the "master teacher" referred to in other reports. The decision to train teachers as building leaders and create school-based teams would ensure that hundreds of teachers and thousands of pupils would benefit from the program. Building on the expertise gained by graduates of the specialization program, the leadership project proposed to choose the most outstanding of these teachers and use them as the core around which to build a cadre of teacher leaders dedicated to implementing the recommendations of the NCTM *Standards* in elementary and middle schools. (When the program was first developed in

1985-86, it anticipated the recommendations of the National Council of Teachers of Mathematics' *Curriculum and Evaluation Standards* and *Professional Standards for Teaching Mathematics*. After the documents were published in 1989 and 1991, they were adopted as "textbooks" for the participants and as the criteria by which program instructors and speakers were selected and evaluated.)

In addition to creating a cadre of mathematics lead teachers at the elementary and middle school level, the program's goals were

1. To help schools upgrade mathematics instruction through the establishment of mathematics resource teams;

2. To integrate mathematics and science with other curriculum areas;

3. To attract high school and college mathematics and science majors, especially women and minorities, to careers in teaching; and

4. To stimulate student interest in and enthusiasm for mathematics and thereby to improve their performance.

Content was at the heart of the program. It was felt that while a teacher must know more than he or she teaches, a *leader* has to see the relationships that exist in the whole spectrum of mathematics at all levels and to identify the underlying, unifying threads that run from kindergarten through high school. A leader also requires the vision to see mathematics applications in other curriculum areas and in the students' world outside the school. The design of the mathematics content included active participation of previous program graduates, instructors, and site directors; school district mathematics coordinators; members of the university's mathematics department and science division; and the Chief of the Bureau of Mathematics Education, New York State Education Department. Recommended coursework included:

- Topics in Discrete Mathematics

- A Problem-Solving Approach to the History of Mathematics

- Mathematical Modeling: Applications to Life Situations

- Algebra and Geometry

- An Introduction to Calculus

- Integration of Mathematics and Science

- Psychology of Learning Mathematics

- Computer Applications for the Mathematics Classroom

The same group was involved in and designed the program's two other components, mathematics education and leadership. The mathematics education component included questioning strategies, setting goals and objectives, guided discovery, principles of research, textbook evaluation and selection, modeling methods and approaches, evaluating learning processes, and issues in mathematics and science education.

The sessions on evaluating an individual student's learning processes were significant on two counts. The method presented, which stressed a continuous dialogue between teacher and student as the student engaged in a specific mathematical activity, was designed to encourage the student to verbalize the actual thought processes involved in the activity. Thus the teacher could identify not only any possible problem but also the exact point in the process at which the problem occurred. Remediation and modification could thus be directed to that point in order to achieve the greatest effect. In a broader vein, this evaluation process was a critical element in helping non-minority teachers develop methods for listening not to what their minority students *said* but to what they *meant*. All too often these teachers needed to become familiar with the social, cultural, and linguistic differences between their students and themselves. The degree of privacy and lack of stress inherent in the evaluation sessions provided excellent opportunities for this to happen.

The leadership component included modeling lessons, stages of cognitive and affective development, principles of staff development, group dynamics, teacher as change agent, and learning theories.

Content was studied in five-week sessions in the program's three summers. Since the mathematics education and leadership components did not lend themselves easily to a university course structure delivered over one semester, these "courses" spanned the three years and activities involved lectures, lesson modeling, and supervision and observation within the schools. The director coordinated, participated in, and monitored the various activities and the many instructors, school people, and special consultants involved in their delivery.

In both summer and academic year sessions, blocks of time were provided for these activities to be meaningfully developed and reflected upon by the participants. Speakers were carefully chosen for their expertise and willingness to spend time with the participants. Many of them joined the participants for classes, activities, and meals and informally exchanged ideas and concerns with them throughout the day. The *Standards* study came alive when Shirley Frye, past president of NCTM, gave the introductory session and spent two days with the participants. Other speakers, including Zalman Usiskin, Seymour Papert, Florence Fasanelli, Gene Maeroff, Henry Pollak, and Genevieve Knight, addressed topics which included:

- Mathematics and Children's Literature
- Mathematics at the Zoo
- Mathematics Developed through Science Activities
- History of Mathematics
- Educational Challenges for the Year 2000

- Mathematics and At-risk Students
- The Mathematics of Basketball

This close contact with recognized leaders was an opportunity most classroom teachers never have the chance to experience and helped give the participants the confidence they needed to become effective leaders. As one participant said,

> Because of the innumerable people we have met who are influential in the field of mathematics, it has given me a new sense of confidence for making inroads in the teaching of mathematics in the school. The confidence and broadening that I have gained in the field of mathematics has empowered me to talk with new teachers about their teaching in general and teaching of mathematics and science specifically.

Leadership abilities were further enhanced through sessions dealing with schoolwide implementation of the *Standards*, mentoring other teachers, choosing textbooks, developing curriculum materials, critiquing lessons, working with student volunteers, working with parents, and developing effective presentation techniques. During the summer sessions, participants were called upon to present sessions for their colleagues similar to those they were expected to do in their schools in the academic year. By the end of the first summer, they were also eligible to attend professional conferences with the ultimate goal of organizing and presenting their own mathematics education conference at the end of the program.

Changes in the way mathematics was taught demanded that curriculum material reflect that change. Development of such material played a large part of the summer programs. After studying the relationship of mathematics to other content areas--sports, the arts, and aspects of everyday life--the participants created curriculum material integrating mathematics into other areas of elementary and middle school study. This material was first field tested in their own classrooms, then shared with their colleagues, and finally compiled for broader distribution. In the same manner, the changing emphasis from product-to-process-oriented learning necessitated the need for new forms of evaluation and assessment, which the participants developed and field tested. In this way the knowledge they gained in the program was spread far beyond their own classrooms and schools in practical, applicable ways.

Academic Year Activities

After each summer of study, participants returned to their schools to utilize the knowledge and skills they acquired. Time was guaranteed through district commitments for implementation of several program projects which provided effective ways of doing this.

Academic year meetings took place once a month, with the districts releasing participants to attend daylong sessions at the university. During these meetings progress on various school activities was reviewed and new areas introduced, including study of learning styles, development of expertise in conducting learning evaluations, and the design of evaluation tools for use in participants' classrooms and in those of selected colleagues. The meetings also provided continuing support and opportunities for networking between participants, staff, and guest speakers. Leading mathematicians, scientists, and educators addressed the group. As a result, the participants were able to keep current on trends in these areas.

School mathematics resource teams were the primary channels through which participants implemented change and raised the level of mathematics education within entire schools. Organized and chaired by the participants, the teams consisted of teachers from various grade levels, specialists, administrators, district coordinators, and, in some cases, parents and upper-grade students. Designed to meet the needs of the individual schools, teams were responsible for selecting textbooks, developing curriculum and material, sponsoring mathematics fairs and contests, publishing mathematics newsletters and magazines, providing workshops for parents, and even restructuring an elementary school to focus on mathematics, science, and technology.

Teachers nurturing teachers was critical to the program. Once familiar with mathematics content and the latest recommendations for effective teaching, participants shared their knowledge with colleagues through staff workshops, demonstration lessons, informal conferences, and one-to-one mentoring of novice teachers. As part of the school and district commitment to create positions of leadership for participants, schedule adjustments provided time for these activities and made it possible for each to have a significant impact on the mathematics teaching of an entire school.

Dr. Henry Pollak, past vice chair of the Mathematical Sciences Education Board, commented on the effectiveness of this activity in an address to the participants:

> The only way really to improve mathematics education in the United States—as *"Everybody Counts"* the NCTM *Standards*, and *Project 2061* are challenging us to do—is for teachers to teach other teachers. This leadership program is a superb model of this, and proof that it really works.

Family Learning and Mathematical Explorations (FLAME) sessions were developed by participants based, in part, on their exposure to EQUALS/FAMILY MATH activities and were an exciting means of involving students and their parents in mathematical discoveries. The sense of accomplishment gained by working together to solve "nontraditional" mathematics problems created a bond between student and parent that strengthened the student's future work in mathematics. Participants presented sessions for schools and districts in the New York metropolitan area, for high school students working with younger students, and for teachers from the Albuquerque/Los Lunas/Bernalillo Public Schools.

Field testing curriculum material focused on the integration of mathematics with other subject areas. As participants explored these relationships in summer mathematics courses designed especially for them, they developed lessons and units for their own classrooms. The material was then field tested during the academic year and the results reviewed and necessary refinements made at monthly meetings. (The tested lessons and units are being compiled and printed for distribution to educators across the country.)

Staff visits were scheduled with each participant, within their schools, several times a year. During these visits, the staff member had an opportunity to see the participant teaching mathematics, to share in staff development activities, to give demonstration lessons, and to talk with administrators about specific ways the program could help meet the individual mathematics needs of the school. Meetings were also scheduled with principals and superintendents to provide a channel for instant feedback.

Attendance at local, regional, and national mathematics education conferences was encouraged as a means of ensuring professional growth and development. During the course of the program each participant was asked to attend a conference with the director and was often asked to assist in a presentation. By the end of the program, many of the teachers were making presentations on their own.

The Student Volunteer Network (SVN) was designed to attract mathematically talented high school students to careers in teaching, *especially those from underrepresented minority groups,* and has grown dramatically since its inception in 1988. Working with elementary students under the supervision of institute-trained teachers, volunteers have gained valuable experience as mathematics teaching assistants. Their duties in the classroom included:

- One-to-one tutoring

- Small group supervision

- Materials development

- Mathematics newsletter/magazine editing

- Videotaping

- Mathematics fair participation
- Lesson development and presentation
- Computer assistance

Volunteers have come from college, high school, junior high school, and even upper-elementary grades. The network is currently in place in several districts in the metropolitan New York area and has been adapted by a university in the southeast. Some universities have recognized the importance of the program by providing scholarships to qualified network graduates. In the first two years, over 80 percent of the New York City volunteers came from minority groups.

A mathematics education conference was organized and presented by the participants as their culminating activity and a means of increasing their impact on the quality of mathematics education in New York City. The daylong conference was attended by over 200 New York City educators and mathematicians. It featured presentations by the program participants; a keynote address by Henry Pollak; a luncheon talk by Fred Paul, Chief, New York State Bureau of Mathematics Education; and a panel of mathematicians, scientists, and educators addressing the critical issue of attracting historically underrepresented groups to the fields of mathematics and science. The panel included Dr. Melvin Webb and Dr. James Mitchell, head of the Analytical Chemistry Research Department for Bell Labs.

Value for At-Risk Students

While it is believed that increasing the level of mathematics teaching benefits *all* students, it is a fact that in the New York City area the majority of those students are from historically underrepresented groups and would be the chief beneficiaries of the program. Approximately 75 percent of the students in the ten districts served by the leadership program were either Hispanic or African American. In five of these districts, the minority student population was over 95 percent.

Clearly, providing these districts with teachers who are effective in the classroom and capable of raising the level of mathematics teaching in schools and districts would have a tremendous impact on the students most in need of encouragement and support.

If more of these teachers were from the same minority groups—and were women, as well—their impact would be even further enhanced. While programs like the specialization and leadership programs depended on district commitment and nominations for their source of applicants, the institute consistently stressed the need for greater minority representation in mathematics and science teaching, and districts responded by submitting more and more qualified minority applicants. Many of these applicants had themselves faced the problems that now confront their students. Once they had mastered the content and developed their leadership skills, these teachers became truly dynamic role models for their students. One student wrote,

> The other day the assistant principal came to ask Miss_____
> to do a math workshop for the other teachers. It's really
> weird to see a black lady showing everyone what to do. But
> it makes me think maybe being a math expert isn't such a
> bad thing if it could get the kind of respect Miss_____ has.

In their classrooms they were able to combine content knowledge with their own experiences to reach students at their own levels and inspire them to grow far beyond. Students commented on the results:

> I like the way Mr._____ helps us learn math. He gives us
> things to do and lets us talk to each other and find the math
> in each activity. Not only does he speak my language
> [Spanish] but he makes me want to speak his
> [mathematics].

> My other teachers had never pushed me to do math because
> "girls don't need to do it." Mrs._____ expects *all* of us to do
> well, even us girls, and she won't accept any excuses. She
> says we won't get anywhere without it and if *she* can do it,

we can do it. At first I didn't believe her, but she made it so exciting that after a while I forgot how much I didn't like it and now I really *can* do it.

At times, their success even amazed the participants. One wrote at the end of her first year in the program:

I thought I was doing a good job. The kids were enthusiastic and looked forward to math class and even began a sort of competition to see who could find mathematics in other places. When the test scores came back this spring, I realized I hadn't done a good job—I'd done a *great* job. Or rather, my kids had. I've never seen so much obvious improvement in one class before. But the real thrill was to watch the kids' faces as they worked and see excitement and satisfaction where there used to be fear and tension.

As participants, many of these teachers brought to the program firsthand knowledge of the educational challenges facing at-risk students. They were able to share their experiences and insights and became excellent resources as the group developed teaching materials and strategies.

Aside from providing at-risk students with as many highly trained mathematics teachers as possible, the leadership program had two components designed specifically to address the needs of this group: the Student Volunteer Network and the Family Learning and Mathematical Exploration (FLAME) sessions.

Student Volunteer Network

It is of primary importance to address the mathematics needs of underrepresented students as early in their educational career as possible. Hence those students will not have an immediate effect on minority representation in the mathematics/science/technology pipeline. The Student Volunteer Network (SVN) helped to address this short-range issue.

The SVN was designed to recruit interested high school students and place them in the classrooms of exemplary mathematics teachers as "teaching assistants." Particular attention was given to selecting girls and minority students in an effort to provide elementary students with positive role models young enough for them to truly identify with. (Over 80 percent of the Volunteers to date have been from minority groups.)

As the program evolved, volunteers were selected from a variety of unanticipated sites. In addition to regular high schools, they also came from two alternative high school programs with nontraditional schedules and from a Boy Scouts of America Explorer Post chartered to the institute for that express purpose. From whatever source they came, all volunteers attended orientation and training sessions before being placed in elementary classrooms and were continually mentored by their assigned teacher. For those with strong mathematics backgrounds, teachers provided enrichment experiences for the volunteers while the volunteers brought new insights and enthusiasm to the elementary mathematic sessions. A few of the volunteers from the alternative schools had weak academic backgrounds. For them, the mentoring relationship helped improve their own mathematics performance while giving them a chance to share what they did know with the younger students.

In addition to working in the classrooms, volunteers were provided with opportunities to experience university life through special training sessions, lectures, and mini-courses on campus. They were exposed to "real world" mathematics through visits to facilities like the Brookhaven National Laboratory and the New York Hall of Science. Activities such as these were an important step in convincing at-risk students that they could take their place in the academic world and find success and satisfaction in the world of mathematics, science, and technology. They also gave the volunteers an opportunity to see the broad range of careers open to those with a solid mathematics background and offered them alternative career choices.

As teachers and schools outside the institute program became interested in having volunteers, arrangements were made for staff members to conduct training sessions for both volunteers and mentor-teachers. For the program to have maximum effect, the mentor-teacher had to demonstrate effective methods and have a firm grasp of mathematics content so that the volunteers would be exposed to exemplary role models.

When originally planned, it was envisioned that the volunteers would be released from high school to work in the elementary school. While many schools did release students for social service credit and others, like the alternative schools, provided even more time than was originally anticipated, some volunteers were not able to work during school hours. They worked, instead, at after-school centers, Saturday academies, and parent workshops. In all cases, volunteers assisted in a variety of ways from helping develop materials and special lessons, to editing newsletters, to working with small groups on specific exploration activities. Not only did they provide role models with whom the younger children could relate, they helped whole families see that it was possible to succeed in mathematics and to enjoy doing so.

Their impact on elementary students has been positive. Excerpts from children's letters indicate the feelings they have about both the volunteers and mathematics:

> If _____ thinks math is important enough to spend his free time doing it with us, it must be worth studying. He seems to like the work so much that he makes us like it, too--even when he's not there.

> It's easy to ask _____ questions when I get stuck. She's like my big sister, not like my teacher, and she remembers what it was like to be in fifth grade and have trouble with math. Math is fun this year with Mrs. _____ and part of the reason is having _____ come to work with us every Tuesday.

The volunteers reflected on their own feelings in journals they kept.

Working with Mrs. _____'s class is the best part of the week. It's neat to watch the kids faces when they finally understand a new concept. I'd like to do this all the time.

While I was helping ____ with his work, Mr. ____ was helping *me* with mine! Geometry seems so much easier when he let's me talk things through till they make sense. I'd like to help kids learn the way he does.

Family Learning and Mathematics Exploration Sessions

Another program component designed to have an impact on at-risk students was aimed at involving the students' families in mathematics explorations. Based, in part, on EQUALS/FAMILY MATH activities that were adapted, extended, and added to by each participant in the leadership program, the FLAME sessions were held at several schools both after school and on Saturdays. They involved students from third through sixth grades with parents, grandparents, aunts, uncles, and older brothers and sisters. Once exposed to mathematics in a nonthreatening manner, the majority of those attending the sessions took a more active role in their children's studies and were eager to go further themselves. The sessions served as springboards for the development of others as several parents asked for mathematics content sessions, training in strategies to help their children understand specific topics, and sessions on career awareness in mathematics and science. Parents in one inner-city school wanted to know if sessions could be run addressing "household survival math"--keeping budgets, balancing checkbooks, figuring out unit prices, etc.

The preceding activities, while developed as components of the leadership program, could just as easily be incorporated with the retraining and specialization programs once a corps of exemplary mathematics teachers was in place. By the same token, the leadership program's focus could be redirected to the creation of master science teachers and the SVN and FLAME sessions correspondingly refocused. In any of these events, great care must be taken to maintain the integrity of each component, of the relationships among the components and of the program as a whole.

Impact in the Schools

Graduates of all three programs have returned to the classroom with the content knowledge and teaching and leadership skills not only to raise the level of mathematics learning in their own classrooms but in those of their colleagues as well. Independent program evaluators found that the performance of participants' students improved. To cite just two of many examples, in one inner-city sixth grade class, 13% had scored above the mean on the previous year's fifth grade MAT mathematics test--at the end of sixth grade, more than 50 percent scored above. In a class of thirty-two third graders of mainly Hispanic background, all but one scored below the 35th percentile on the second grade MAT test. Fifteen scored above it on the third grade test and five of those scored above the 70th percentile.

Exposure to learning through problem solving, to the history of mathematics, to the many applications of mathematics in other areas, to the development of curriculum integrating mathematics with other content areas, to cooperative group work, and to the psychology of learning mathematics gives participants an arsenal of weapons to use in the battle for their students' future. These tools are even more effective because they were gained not through lecture but through experience. Program participants returned to their classrooms with new visions. One evaluator noted that they

> encourage children to hypothesize, employ inquiry techniques, use scientific methodology and record data. The teachers model problem-solving techniques and are willing to share their strategies with colleagues and pupils.

In short, the participants teach their classes as they were taught in the programs. They impart their own enthusiasm and excitement about mathematics and provide positive role models for their students, as evidenced by student letters to the institute director:

She remembered what she learned and taught it better. When she was having a test and she was nervous, we would tell her not to worry and to have confidence in herself.

I liked it when my teacher went to school because she was able to teach us the things she learned there. Our marks in math and science improved because of that.

My scores were the highest they have ever been! . . .so I think it is a great idea that teachers go to school.

I felt good when I learned that adults got nervous on their tests as well as children. She learned math and science and she told us some of the things she learned. . . . She became teacher of the year and she was very happy.

The participants' impact was also recognized by district superintendents:

. . .we have benefitted in several ways. . .the courses which enrich participants' backgrounds. . .they translate their new expertise into practical application...the teacher training component afforded us the opportunity to have them share their knowledge with colleagues.

Recently I was asked to take over a junior high school in another district as an emergency measure to raise the academic achievement level of the students and to improve the teaching of the staff. I was able to undertake such an extraordinary responsibility because one of the program participants was able to take over the math curriculum and train all the teachers.

The program helped to galvanize the school, . . .Participants generated a lot of involvement from their colleagues and helped improve students' mathematics achievement. . . .

The participant has become both symbolically and substantially a true resource to other teachers. . .and the district plans to extend her role to become involved with parents. As a result of the program there is belief among teachers that the district is committed to using inside people as resources. The participant plays a key role in reshaping district policy; it is no longer a top-down administrative fiat.

By principals:

She embraced an opportunity to go beyond the norm and enhance her mathematical skills and understanding and then transferred those learnings to her peers and students.

By colleagues:

Her classroom is what the textbooks recommend all teachers strive to accomplish. Her energy level and dedication far surpass anyone's given imagination. She models her instructional strategies to the new teachers. She does any and all things to increase the mathematical learning of the students. She is an *educator*.

And by the participants themselves:

It may seem inconsequential to be raving about the chance to discuss math education with another math teacher; but in the past it has been a rare occasion for an elementary and secondary teacher to really pursue our mutual interest in depth. My present opportunity has enabled me to serve as a turnkey in sharing concerns, techniques, and knowledge with each level.

Challenge for the Future

Although minority participation was high in the three programs and, as a result of their participation, many minority teachers became leaders in their schools, they are disheartened by the situation which still prevails in the general education community. Two participants' comments on conferences they attended point up their concern:

It's my hope to meet people [at the conference] who will influence and encourage my own mathematics teaching so the benefits of the conference will be passed on to my own students. *It's also my hope to meet other minority teachers and to discuss common problems and solutions with them. It would be wonderful if minority representation was large, but I suspect such will not be the case.*

The most disturbing aspect of the entire conference was the fact that excluding myself, I could count only nine other black people among the six hundred in attendance. If so few minority persons are in attendance at a major national conference, then indeed the amount of persons available for role models for minority youngsters is very limited.

Unfortunately, this situation is representative of the educational population as a whole and will continue to be so until the change effected by programs such as these is reflected in similar programs across the country. The situation will continue until more and more institutions and school systems, when addressing the needs of minority students, heed the advice of organizations like AAAS and begin, as the institute programs have done, to

- Provide the best teachers
- Reform the curriculum
- Set high expectations
- Develop plans to raise achievement levels
- Guide minorities into academic tracks
- Involve parents
- Encourage the pursuit of mathematics and science fields
- Enhance teacher professionalism and cultural sensitivity (AAAS, 1989)

If each tries to solve the whole problem, we'll get nowhere; if we all do what we can, where we can, together we can change the future. If institutions and school systems across the country collaborate in the development of mathematics— or science—programs such as these, if minority enrollment in them is encouraged, if minority teachers return to their classrooms as positive role models for students who will go on to further study in mathematics and science and perhaps return to the classroom as teachers themselves—perhaps a conference attendee will never again be able to count the number of minority participants on two hands. And perhaps the term "historically underrepresented groups" in mathematics and science can become simply an historical term, no longer applicable to a generation where numeracy multiplies achievement rather than one where innumeracy divides the "haves" from the "have nots."

References

American Association for the Advancement of Science. (1989). *Making Mathematics and Science Work for Hispanics.* Washington, DC.

---. (1989). *Phase 1 Reports.* Washington, DC.

Carnegie Forum on Education and the Economy. (1986). *A Nation Prepared: Teachers for the 21st Century.* Report of the Task Force on Teaching as a Profession. New York: Carnegie Corporation.

Conference Board for Mathematical Sciences. (1984). *New Goals for Mathematical Science Educator.* Washington, DC.

National Council of Teachers of Mathematics. (1989). *Curriculum and Evaluation Standards for School Mathematics.* Reston, VA.

National Research Council. (1989). *Everybody Counts: A Report to the Nation on the Future of Mathematics Education.* Washington, DC: National Academy Press.

National Science Board. (1982). "National Science Commission Report on Precollege Education in Mathematics, Science and Technology." Washington, DC.

3. Teaching Mathematics through Context: Unleashing the Power of the Contextual Learner

Everard Barrett

In June 1976, twenty fifth, twenty-six sixth, and five seventh grade students from the socioeconomically depressed minority community of Roosevelt, Long Island, took the 1976 New York State Regents Examination in Ninth Year Algebra. They achieved a much higher level than the ninth graders in the same school district who took the same exam. Sixty-seven percent of the younger group passed as compared to the 25% rate of passing grades among the ninth graders. All forty-six fifth and sixth graders attended the Theodore Roosevelt Elementary School.

In September 1983, thirty-four fifth graders from another low socioeconomic environment, Bedford-Stuyvesant, Brooklyn, took the 1983 version of the same examination. Sixty-three percent of them passed, with six scoring 90 percent or higher.

This level of mathematical achievement by such large numbers of youngsters in one elementary school is without precedent in the history of mathematics education anywhere in the United States. In fact, since the Japanese teach Algebra I to their seventh graders, these accomplishments may be without precedent worldwide.

In the Washington Elementary School, Mount Vernon, New York, third grade students averaged three-months gain in their math scores for each month of instruction based on their performance on the 1978 SRA (Science Research Associates) test. Comparison of average pre- and post-percentile rankings showed a growth of 45 percentage points in less than one year. The second graders gained an average of 2.7 months for each month of instruction. The Washington School is situated in a low socioeconomic section of Mount Vernon.

Within the schools of Cold Spring Harbor, New York, an affluent community on the north shore of Long Island, second, third, and fourth graders gained an average of 21, 23, and 21 percentage points, respectively, on the California Test of Basic Skills, after having only one year of exposure to the Barrett method. As of May 1979, the average second, third, fourth, and fifth grade students in Cold Spring Harbor scored at the 84th, 86st and 85th percentile, respectively, on the CTBS. The grade equivalent averages were 3.5 for the second graders; 5.4 for the third graders; 6.4 for the fourth graders; and 8.1 for the fifth graders. Those students who scored below the 50th percentile on the CTBS pre-test (1977-1978) averaged at the 33rd percentile. In less than one year, those same students averaged at the 67th percentile. This statistical information shows dramatic increases in scores that were already above the national average.

The author has been making yearly interventions in numerous public school systems from 1973 to the present. More recent data will be presented later in the text.

How did all this happen? What were the theoretical notions which made this possible? What were the compelling awarenesses which so effectively transformed the teachers' perspectives on the teaching of mathematics and, consequently, their pedagogical strategies and techniques in their own classrooms? What did teachers do that was different? The purpose of this chapter is to (1) present the author's theoretical and pedagogical ideas which inspired his successful interventions, (2) provide readers some practical strategies and techniques which demonstrate some applications, and (3) discuss some implications.

Learners in thousands of classrooms throughout our nation (particularly youth at risk) have difficulty understanding and retaining mathematics. But do they experience difficulty in understanding and retaining stories? If they do not, then it might be useful to inquire about the basis of this phenomenon and its implications for mathematics education (Barrett, 1989).

Because teachers have strongly encouraged students to memorize in order to retain mathematics, we might begin our inquiry by asking whether memorization is the means whereby even the slowest learners retain stories. This is clearly not the case, since we know that children tell stories "in their own words," which are not the same as those they heard when they were told the story originally. What, then, is this powerful mental capacity in all of us which makes retention of a story inevitable?

If you seriously engage yourself in an effort to recall a story you heard in the past, you will find that, in effect, your mind is "piecing it together" even as you tell it. Behavioral psychologists refer to this phenomenon as "chaining." You are able to do this as a consequence of the cause-and-effect relationships your mind perceived, as you heard it the first few times. You noted how a buildup of circumstances would cause an event which, in turn, would become part of a larger set of circumstances, which again would lead to another event and thus the story unfolded. Was not your effort to recall a story one of reconstruction rather than memorization?

What do the words "prince" and "slippers" trigger in your mind? These entities, as experienced by our psyche, are woven together in a contextual structure entitled "Cinderella." With the exception of a very small number of brain-damaged individuals, every human mind is capable of reconstructing a whole story from a few entities within some context. This is what permits us to say we know the story and, more importantly, to know that we know it.

We all have the experience of seeing a face and noting its familiarity but never the less asking, "Who is that?" What cognitive activity occurs in our minds so that we might reconstruct the person's identity? It is when that face triggers a few associations such as a particular high school, a certain incident, a certain person. These associations trigger the recollection of much additional, contextually related information. This contextual type of knowing permits us to declare with confidence and with the "certification" of internal authority, "I see!" "I understand!" "I know!" "This makes sense!"

By the age of three to four years, virtually all children have taught themselves a "foreign language." The average six-year-old already understands between 8,000 and 14,000 words (Carey, 1977). The first language that babies encounter is foreign in the sense that they did not know it at birth. Consider the fact that the meanings of many words they comprehend were neither looked up in a dictionary nor explained by Mom. Besides the meanings of words, they acquired meanings of phrases and sentences. Do you remember, as a teenager (or even quite recently), deciphering the meaning of a word or a phrase based on how it was used in some conversation? Was this not an example of contextual learning? That children function in this manner to master a language at such an early age is as much true for slow learners as it is for quick ones. They function the same way since both use context as a means for acquiring language and retaining stories.

Whenever any human mind perceives, for the first time, a link between two entities, however irrelevant or insignificant each one had become, this discovery is sufficiently significant to immediately attract the total preoccupation of the mind (however briefly) from all other conscious activities. For example, both the barking of the dog and the arrival of the mail carrier may have become insignificant to a child prior to the discovery of the dynamic between them, whereby the barking informs him or her that the mail carrier has arrived. A link of any kind between two or more entities is of intrinsic and irresistible interest to all human beings (Bruner, 1963). It is the moment of connection, of understanding, of transforming so as to produce new insight. Piaget's (1970) notion of equilibration as a search for a balance between a child's cognitive structure and his or her perceptions may be another appropriate frame of reference through which we might view this phenomenon. It is impossible for anyone to function in human society without this capacity.

It is clear from the above examples that the cognitive capacity to reconstruct a whole contextual structure from a few entities within it (a type of cognitive activity which is highly esteemed in academic society) belongs to even the slowest learners you have ever seen. This is one of our endowments. It belongs to us by virtue of merely being human. It ensures the retention of much contextually related information found in everyone's experiences.

Consequently, the reality is

> that every child was a competent contextual learner before going to school. The proof of this statement is that every child, with extremely few brain-damaged exceptions, taught himself/herself a language at an early age and retained stories after hearing them a few times. It is well known that the predominant cognitive functioning necessary for such accomplishments is the construction of relationships within some context; otherwise called contextual learning. (Barrett, 1990)

If slow learners have the capacity to retain contextually related information, can it be activated to facilitate the learning and retention of mathematics? Is the view of context in a story also present, for example, in the teaching of long division or transforming a fraction into an equivalent decimal? In examining the traditional algorithm for transforming the fraction 5/8 to an equivalent decimal,

$$8\overline{\smash{\big)}\,5}$$

the teacher says, "Eight cannot go into five once, so you must place a decimal point next to five and immediately above it." Why? "Just do it!" The teacher continues, "Place some zeros next to the decimal point." How many? "A few." He continues, "Eight can't go into five but eight goes into fifty." It should be noted that to replace five with fifty is a falsehood. "Eight into fifty is six," he says while writing six next to the decimal point in the quotient. This, again, is a falsehood: that is six-tenths, not six. "Eight times six is forty-eight." Another falsehood: that is not forty-eight. "Forty-eight from fifty is two." That is not two. The work now appears on the blackboard as follows:

$$\begin{array}{r} .6 \\ 8\overline{)5.000} \\ \underline{4\;8} \\ 2 \end{array}$$

He continues, "Bring down a zero." Why? "That's how you get the right answer." Have you ever heard a meaningful explanation for "bring down"? "Eight into twenty is two," he says while writing two in the hundredths' place of the quotient. Another falsehood: that's not two. Need more be said? This dialogue by the teacher is composed entirely of falsehoods and meaningless statements.

Clearly it is impossible for a pupil to exercise his or her capacity as a competent contextual learner when taught long division or transformation of a fraction to a decimal (using division) by means of traditional techniques. The author recalls that as a youngster he "broke through" in his attempt to master long division soon after it suddenly occurred to him: "It is not possible to understand that stuff." How strange! It was necessary to "abandon reason" as a prerequisite to mastering the skill. It was impossible to see, contextually, how each "step" in the algorithm was related to the objective of the long division exercise (Barrett, 1990). In fact, we had no choice but to suppress that part of our psyche which, by virtue of how we are created, yearns for meaning and understanding. That part of our psyche has a very important name in education. It is called intelligence. We suppressed intelligence in order to "learn" the traditional long division algorithm (Barrett, 1989). This statement also applies to the learning of all arithmetical algorithms as traditionally taught.

Much research in cognitive psychology supports this contention. Early work by Garner (1966) brought about the conclusion that

> People do perceive properties of sets of stimuli and these properties affect ease of learning. But the stimuli must be presented so that it is clear to the subject what constitutes a single class, group or subset. If the stimuli are presented so that the subject must learn them as individual stimuli, he can do so, but then he cannot take advantage of some facilitating properties of sets.

Many other researchers (Ausubel, 1968; Battig, 1968; Rohwer and Levin, 1968) have concluded that it is not the repetition of discrete facts that leads to efficient learning but, rather, the coherence of presentation within a meaningful context. Therefore, it should not be a surprise to find that researchers, such as Vaidya and Chansky (1980), have demonstrated that children who understand concepts such as classification and seriation perform best on tests of mathematical ability.

The author's response to this problem is being implemented in many school systems. Various algorithms of arithmetic and the dialogues associated with their performance were modified so that, with huge gains in efficiency, meaning will always precede the acquisition of the various skills and will always be experienced throughout their performance (Barrett, 1979).

The modification of the preceding algorithm for transforming five eighths to an equivalent decimal follows. After placing five as the dividend and eight as the divisor, pupils are made aware that since eight cannot "go into five once," they must move from the ones' place in the quotient over to the tenths' place. However, it is not possible to fill the tenths' place (in the quotient) unless we change the dividend to tenths. Hence we must "exchange" five wholes (symbolized as 5) for fifty tenths (symbolized as 5.0). Now we can say, "Eight into fifty tenths is six tenths." Having said that, we write ".6" in the quotient (the decimal point in the quotient directly above the decimal point in the dividend). Continuing, we say, "Eight times six tenths are forty-eight tenths." We now write forty-eight tenths, symbolized as 4.8, below 5.0 (the decimal points "lined up") and subtract forty-eight tenths from fifty tenths. The difference is two tenths, symbolized as .2, and written below the 4.8 (the decimal points lined up). "We now have to fill the hundredths' place in the quotient." This cannot be done until we change the new dividend, two tenths (.2), into hundredths. So we exchange two tenths for twenty hundredths (.20). Continuing, we say, "Eight into twenty hundredths is two hundredths," and place the digit two in the hundredths' place of the quotient. "Eight times two hundredths are sixteen hundredths," so we write sixteen hundredths (.16) under the twenty hundredths (.20) appropriately (decimals in line) and subtract. "Sixteen hundredths from twenty hundredths leaves four hundredths." Four hundredths must be written symbolically as .04 under .16. Continuing similarly, we must exchange four hundredths (.04) for forty thousandths (.040) in order to "fill" the thousandths' place in the quotient. Since the new dividend is represented numerically as .040, we say, "Eight into forty thousandths are five thousandths," and write the digit 5 in the thousandths' place of the quotient. Five eighths are equivalent to .625.

Please note that in direct contrast to the traditional algorithm, every statement made by the teacher in the modified algorithm is true. The completed example appears below (Barrett, 1979):

```
        .625
      _____
   8 | 5 . 0
     -4 . 8
      _____
       .20
      -.16
      _____
       .040
      -.040
      _____
          0
```

Is there a view of context here? It is possible for any learner to see that the "maximum tenths" of eight which can be subtracted from fifty tenths (5.0) is six (tenths of eight); the "maximum hundredths" of eight which can be subtracted from twenty hundredths (.20) is two (hundredths of eight); and the "maximum thousandths" of eight which can be subtracted from forty thousandths is five (thousandths of eight).

This contextual vision virtually guarantees delivery of meaning prior to pupils' acquisition of skill in performing the transformation of a fraction to an equivalent decimal. When pupils are taught arithmetical algorithms by means of falsehoods and meaningless statements, the opposite occurs: skill precedes meaning. In fact, for the rest of one's life following the acquisition of skill by traditional means, meaning is a rare occurrence among the vast majority of individuals. Whenever children acquire this "contextual view" of an arithmetical algorithm prior to the acquisition of skill, meaning will also be experienced concurrently every time the skill is being performed.

With tremendous gains in efficiency, any arithmetical algorithm can be performed by youngsters in such a manner that they see each step, even each thought, as related to the overall objective of the exercise. Accordingly, the author has made alterations on arithmetical algorithms in order to accommodate the contextual view; so that the competent contextual learners can master mathematics as inevitably as they mastered their native language or retention of stories (Barrett, 1990).

Will this approach guarantee the learning and retention of the algorithms in the same way that context guarantees the learning and retention of a story? Documentation is available with respect to the performance of long division (up to six-place dividends and three-place divisors) by average second graders. This was achieved by means of the contextual approach. When taught this topic traditionally, poor retention is observable when pupils consistently forget what to do next. They are unable to string all the steps together. The consistently successful performance of long division by the second graders demonstrated that they had learned and retained the modified algorithm. Success was also achieved in training fifth and sixth grade teachers to deliver competence in Algebra I to their classes. On four separate occasions (in four different years), fifth and sixth grade classes passed, with flying colors, the same statewide examination in elementary algebra that was traditionally reserved for the brightest ninth grade students. In fact, during the 1976-77 school year, a sixth grade class, which had mastered algebra in fifth grade, went on to cover 80% of the traditional intermediate algebra and trigonometry curriculum.

Consider what happened every time children were given long division homework. The "inner voice," which we all know, "talked" us through the various steps. This means that all those falsehoods and meaningless statements were repeated by the inner voice over and over again. Consider, also, that this phenomenon continues to be experienced in the performance of many other skills involving operations on fractions and decimals. This is undesirable since the most appropriate mental processes necessary for learning and doing mathematics are very different from those hammered into us for the purpose of "learning" arithmetic!

Prior to our encounter with long division, much of arithmetic made sense. That "three plus two equals five" made sense if we could make one group out of two and count all the objects. That "four times five equals twenty" made sense if we could make one group from four groups of five objects each and count them all. Making sense, at this stage, was consistent with and appropriate to our reality as contextual learners. The contextual view brought comfort and confidence to the learning and doing of mathematics to the same degree as the absence of it brought pain and frustration. We were taken "off track" by noncontextual arithmetical algorithms and classroom dialogues.

The reversal, whereby meaning precedes acquisition of skill and is experienced concurrently as the algorithm is being performed, has profound implications for the teaching of mathematics. Empowered elementary school teachers were able to deliver extraordinary competence in arithmetic and Algebra I to fifth and sixth grade classes in the low socioeconomic communities of Roosevelt and Bedford- Stuyvesant, New York. As a consequence of that fact, the claim is made: all of arithmetic can be mastered by all fourth graders. The author must emphasize that the basis for his claim is the reality of his experience as well as statistical analyses and criterion-referenced data (Stolzberg, 1977, 1979, 1981). It is the outcome of intense and sustained "hands on" staff-development interventions within classrooms over the past eighteen years. Further implications are the following:

1. The tremendous reduction in remediation time and efforts (as well as cost);

2. Elementary school teachers, competent contextual learners that they are, learn to understand arithmetic while learning how to teach it contextually; and

3. The enormous amount of time now made available for non-computational math topics.

Many years ago, the mathematics education establishment, responding to its failure to deliver acceptable levels of student competence in the learning of its various mathematics curricula, prescribed the "spiral" curriculum as the means of solving the problem. Unfortunately, the spiral approach to learning the content of five concentrations (for example, computation, problem solving, geometry, probability, and statistics) in one school year is similar to learning five stories by reading page one of the first, followed by page one of the second, and so on through all of them, before proceeding similarly with the remaining pages. It may also be compared to studying five paintings by dividing each into ten strips, then looking over strip number one of the first, followed by strip number one of the second, and so on through all of them, before proceeding similarly with the remaining strips. No one reads a story or looks at a painting that way. Learners would not be able to achieve contextual vistas in any one of those stories or paintings. A curriculum void of vistas is a "curriculum void" indeed! Curricula will activate and unleash contextual learners to the extent that each offers "clusters" of dynamically related information and is presented to them with the intention of completing a developmental sequence within one before beginning another.

Teaching mathematics contextually not only implies that the teacher possesses the contextual view; it also means that he or she has the ability to consistently articulate contextually within the subject matter. For example, in finding how many twenty-fourths are equivalent to three-fourths, a teacher should never say to new learners of this topic, "Four into twenty-four is six and six times three equals eighteen; so three fourths equal eighteen twenty-fourths." There is very little view of context in this statement. Consider the contextuality of the following dialogue. "Twenty fourths are which members of the fourths' family?" Students respond, "The sixth." "So the sixth numerator in the family is. . . ?" Students respond, "Eighteen." Another example involves the transformation of an improper fraction to a mixed number. Teachers should never say to new learners of this topic, "Seven into twenty-three equals three with a remainder of two; so twenty-three sevenths equals three and two sevenths." Consider the dialogue which follows. "How many sevenths equal one whole?" Students respond, "Seven." "Can you take one whole out of twenty-three sevenths?" Students respond, "Yes." "How many sevenths is that?" "Seven sevenths." "Can you take two wholes out of twenty-three sevenths?" "Yes." "How many sevenths is that?" "Fourteen sevenths." "Can you take three wholes out of twenty-three sevenths?" "Yes." "How many sevenths is that?" "Twenty-one sevenths." "Can you take four wholes out of twenty-three sevenths?" "No." The teacher concludes that three wholes were taken out of twenty-three sevenths and two sevenths were "left over"; so twenty-three sevenths equals three and two sevenths. Internalization of these contextual questions by the learner's inner voice (for repeated applications to such examples in the future) enhances both the retention of and appreciation for the related subject matter. For the purpose of facilitating efforts in cooperative learning, students who articulate subject matter contextually communicate more effectively.

It is important to note that all the examples of accelerated learning described in Roosevelt, and Bedford-Stuyvesant involved only at-risk youth. Particularly valuable to this segment of the population has been the impact of the author's consistently contextual approaches on student's self-esteen, self-image, and motivation. Each participating student acquired a personal discovery of his or her intellect, in the sense that the power of the mind to grasp ideas and relations was activated. Students' teachers had learned how to activate their pre-school competence. Consequently, it is critical that teachers of at-risk youth acquire insights into mathematics as a developmental flow of dynamically related concepts and schemas.

Fortunately, the pedagogy designed to activate competence in students also activates the same in their teachers. They are also competent contextual learners. Among the author's most rewarding recollections, over many years of staff developmental interventions, are the hundreds of occasions that teachers have expressed both surprise and delight in their discovery that there are alternate, and more efficient, arithmetical algorithms which make sense even as they are being performed; that mechanically performed skills can actually have associated meanings which they understand clearly. This awareness brings a sense of relief for many teachers as they remove their burdens of fear, doubt, and avoidance of mathematics. They often exclaim, "Where were you when I needed you?"

Do you recall (as the author does in his own experience) occasions when you were "explaining" long division, for example, and knew your explanations were not making sense? What was your response when a student asked, for example, "Why did you 'bring down'?" In many instances, the teacher's response is, "That's how you get the answer," or, "Just do it." This type of response, of which the author was guilty in the distant past (and it is desirable to distance oneself from such explanations), does not nurture any students in mathematics and is particularly damaging to at-risk youth.

Teaching mathematics contextually, with respect to the internal dynamics of relationships, makes it possible for teachers to consistently "tell the truth" as they, or their students, articulate the development of an algorithm while they are performing it. At-risk students, existing as they often do on the lower rungs of the socioeconomic ladder, with the attendant damage to their self-image and academic motivation, are in dire need of this nurturing. Without it, they have no other alternative than to either deactivate their intelligence (which is almost all they have left), in order to cope with explanations consisting entirely of falsehoods, or simply "tune out."

At the very foundation of the learning of arithmetic is learning of the basic addition, subtraction, multiplication, and division facts. At-risk youth are at a distinct disadvantage, at this level, to those blessed with more fortunate circumstances, since teachers have generally relied on parents to provide the drills necessary for immediate and accurate recall of the facts. The author's pedagogy makes it possible for a teacher to provide an unprecedented acceleration in the delivery of the basic facts to learners:

1. First graders learn all addition and subtraction facts;

2. Second graders learn all multiplication and division facts;

3. First graders learn the higher addition or higher subtraction facts within four days; and

4. Second graders learn a whole multiplication table, and the associated division facts, in thirty minutes.

The above schedule for the mastery of the basic facts, or any reasonable extention thereof, removes them as obstacles and releases an enormous amount of time for non-computational topics in the mathematics curriculum. Given this rate of learning, parents do not have to become teachers, and at-risk youth will not be placed at a huge disadvantage at the very beginning of their experience with mathematics. Please note, however, that consistent with his contextual approach, the author's methodology always provides students a cognitive basis for their knowledge of the facts. Immediate recall is the outcome of rapid-response, mental activity games designed to speed up cognition.

The television screen has a major responsibility for the immense decline in literacy throughout the United States. Will the advent of the calculator in early childhood classrooms have a positive impact on the level of innumeracy? The author believes it is critical that children discover their own minds as calculators before receiving these instruments. There is a cognitive discipline which can be acquired as a result of frequent mental and written training with numbers and their associated operations. This discipline is indispensable to children's future capacity to perform the rigorous algebraic manipulations in high school, which are necessary to students for the mastery of freshman and sophomore calculus in college. Calculus, in turn, is indispensable to students' future development into engineers and MBAs.

Children need a lot of training and practice in performing the basic operations on whole numbers, fractions, and decimals. This is due, in part, to the necessity that they learn to organize their work on paper neatly, effectively, and coherently. Acquisition of these skills in arithmetic tremendously facilitates their development in algebra and, eventually, in calculus. Writing a composition requires an enormous amount of practice. So does "mathematical writing," which begins with "arithmetical writing" followed by "algebraic writing," and so on. There are many talented students in mathematics who were surpassed in performance by less gifted students who simply practiced more. This is as true of mathematics as it is of any other discipline: music, basketball, and chess, to name a few. Sufficiently reducing children's training and practice of computational arithmetic leads eventually to their elimination from competition for the most lucrative job opportunities. The author's proposal for accelerating the learning of computation by presenting the subject matter contextually promises to complete this training by fourth grade.

For some readers, the notion of accelerated learning in mathematics may imply the imposition of pressure on some very unhappy children. It is reasonable to claim that all children are inevitable and accelerated learners of stories since they learn and retain one after hearing it a few times. This is a pleasant experience due to the comfortable assimilation of contextually related information. Similarly, the accelerated learning of mathematics is an inevitable and enjoyable outcome of a pedagogy which consistently activates the contextual learner in every child.

Besides contextual awareness, there are other sources of motivation for the acquisition of skill in computation. One of these is derived from children's necessity to compute in order to solve problems in the real world. This important type of motivation is currently favored by the mathematics education establishment. There is another powerful source of motivation which is as important as any other. It is that which derives from the joy of performance. It can be observed in children when they proclaim newly learned performance with delight. Why do girls play hopscotch? Why do adults work on crossword puzzles? Why do children play with tongue twisters? Why will one child mimic almost anything another does? Often, it is neither what you do nor the real-world application, but the fact that "I can do it, too," which brings satisfaction and, more importantly, self-esteem. Some may argue that children never enjoy computation for its own sake. On the contrary, they immensely enjoy it when the steps they take in its performance make sense. The current stigma associated with computation may have some justification in situations where it is a rote exercise. If we must exclaim, "Down with rote computation!" then with greater fervor let us proclaim, "Up with conceptual computation!" Participants in games derive self esteem from successful experiences in sufficiently challenging situations. When the challenge has been mastered, the game is not worth playing. Since the contextual view accelerates the acquisition of computational skills, the likelihood of boredom is significantly diminished. The author suggests that all forms of motivation should be equally activated in all students.

The author is convinced that if traditional practice in the teaching of arithmetic had not hammered a non-contextual acceptance of arithmetic into our psyches, vast numbers of students and teachers across the nation would not have similarly approached higher levels of mathematics. Our natural endowment for contextual knowledge would have been more likely activated for the learning of mathematics beyond arithmetic, if we had the benefit of contextual teaching.

Not only have students been damaged by their intense and demanding exposure to non-contextual arithmetic but, to the extent that teachers tolerate students' attempts to memorize their way through algebra, trigonometry, and calculus, mathematics education in this nation has become severely incapacitated. Consider, for example, the small number of high school students who discover the joy of starting a problem with "given" information and who, by means of definitions, postulates, and theorems, "trigger off" dynamically related information until a logical pathway to the solution is found. Consider, again, that among the small percentage of students nationwide who survive to the level of trigonometry, only a very small number acquire the satisfaction of seeing the contextual development which derives, for example, the formula for cosine of a difference of two angles. Consider, finally, that among the very small percentage of our student population which survives mathematics to the level of calculus, the majority, in spite of a mechanical competence at determining various limits, do not understand the limit concept and are totally lost with respect to epsilon-delta discussions.

As stated in a previous article of limited circulation which has introduced the author's methodology to some school systems (Barrett, 1990),

> we must consistently present an internal contextual view of mathematics to learners. This view focuses on the internal dynamics of relationships within the subject matter and is at least as important as the view which sees mathematics in its external contextual relationship to the world. It is the predominant means whereby all learners everywhere will acquire competence in mathematics, just as it was the means whereby they learned their native language and retained stories.

In summary, the Barrett Method of Mathematical Instruction is an approach which accelerates the learning of mathematics by activating the competence of the contextual learner in every child. Though the data only support success in elementary grades (K-6), this approach has obvious applicability to teaching mathematics on any level. The following suggestions are developed for teachers who desire to begin using this approach for teaching mathematics.

1. In order to ensure learning and retention of mathematics, teachers must activate the same cognitive means whereby children learn and retain stories: the

human endowment to assimilate contextually related information.

2. It is desirable to teach mathematics in such a way as to cover whole vistas of contextually related information as quickly as possible. Facilitate your efforts by giving patient and thorough contextual explanations which show the linkages among concepts and schemas.

3. Teach mathematics with the awareness that it is best retained by means of reconstruction of contextually related information rather than by memorization.

4. When teaching mathematics, be constantly aware of where your students are as you nurture them along some developmental "journey."

5. Teachers should always be careful to ensure that their classroom articulation clearly conveys an irresistible contextual development of concepts and schemas to the minds of their students.

6. Teachers should consistently require of their students a contextual articulation of mathematical concepts and schemas. This facilitates cooperative learning.

7. When explaining mathematics to students, teachers should be so intellectually honest as to continuously confront themselves (even while explaining) with the question: "Does what I say make sense?" This should be a diligent, ever-present, and ongoing mental exercise as one teaches mathematics.

8. Teach consistently with the objective of conveying mathematics to learners as reconstructible knowledge.

9. Build strong self-esteem in your students by permitting them to experience the sense of power over mathematics which derives from their capacity to reconstruct whole vistas of related information from a few ideas.

10. Consistently ensure that, contrary to traditional practice in mathematics education, meaning always precedes the acquisition of skill.

11. Activate the contextual learner and you activate intelligence.

12. Train the "outer voice" of students to articulate contextually so that the "inner voices" can "talk" them through problems they encounter independently when doing homework or taking tests.

13. Design curricula in mathematics which consist of "clusters" of contextually related concepts and schemas.

14. Use questioning techniques that would contextually related concepts and schemas from students.

15. Achieve accelerated learning of mathematics for all children by teaching the subject matter contextually. As the acceleration evolves, there will be a notable absence of pressure on the learners and a huge diminution of "math anxiety."

Program Assessment of Mathematics through Context

1976-1978

In 1976, 34 out of 51 fifth, sixth, and seventh graders whose mathematics scores had been previously low passed a New York State Board of Regents mathematics test intended for ninth graders. This experience took place in Roosevelt, New York, at the Roosevelt Elementary School.

In 1977, Hempstead, New York, third graders scored an average of 4.3 on the Metropolitan Achievement Test. In Cold Spring Harbor, New York, fourth graders scored 6.2 on the California Achievement Test. Roosevelt second graders scored 4.6 on the Iowa Test of Basic Skills; Glen Cove, New York, third graders scored an average of 4.5 on the California Achievement Test and thirty-three out of fifty-four first graders "topped" the California Achievement Test by achieving the maximum score.

During the 1977-78 school year, the Barrett Method of Mathematical Instruction was offered in the Glen Cove, Hempstead, and Mount Vernon, New York, school districts, grades one through three. The children were pre- and post-tested using either the California Test of Basic Skills or the Metropolitan Achievement Test. Tables 1-4 represents the results of Barrett's instructional strategies.

Table 1. Glen Cove
Grade Equivalent Averages for the Entire Landing School Grades 1-3

Grade	N	(1) Pre-Test G.E. Mean	(2) Post-Test G.E. Mean	(3) Average Gain (in Months)	(4) Average Gain (in Months) per Month
1	54	*	2.4	*	*
2	54	2.0	3.3	13	1.6
3	53	3.3	4.5	13 (rounded	1.6

* No pre-test was administered to the first grade.

This table presents data obtained from the Landing School in Glen Cove. Column 3 refers to the average gain (in months) for participating students in that school during the eight month interval between administrations of the California Achievement Test. Column 4 presents the average gain (in months) for each month of instruction. At grades two and three, this was a 1.6-month increase for each month of instruction.

Since no pre-test was administered to the first grade, a base level was not obtained. The 2.4 grade equivalent average of the post-test is an underestimation, since many of the students scored at the uppermost point on that test.

It is important to note that the achievement test used does not assess knowledge of the advanced concepts which students of the Barrett approach had mastered.

Table 2. Glen Cove
Percentile Averages for the Entire Landing School Grades 1-3

Grade	N	Pre-Test Percentile Mean	Post-Test Percentile Mean	Gain
1	54	*	78	*
2	54	48	73	25
3	53	60	71	11

* No pre-test was administered to the first grade.

As can be seen by reviewing the percentile scores on this table, the average student in each of grades 1, 2, and 3 scored higher than 78, 73, and 71 percent of students in a representative national sample on the post-test.

Table 3. Hempstead
Grade Equivalent Averages

Grade	N	(1) Pre-Test G.E. Mean	(2) Post-Test G.E. Mean	(3) Average Gain (in Months)	(4) Average Gain (in Months) per Month
2	96	2.2	3.3	11	1.6
2	96	2.8	4.3	15	2.2.6

This table presents data obtained in the Hempstead Public School District. Pre-test and post-test data, as well as the average gain in scores over the seven- month interval between administrations of the Metropolitan Achievement Test (column 3), are listed.

In order to place these gains in a standard perspective, column 4 is the average gain per month. By reviewing this column, it is clearly seen that second and third graders gained an average of 1.6 and 2.2 months, respectively, for each of the seven months of instruction.

Table 4. Glen Cove

Grade Equivalent Averages for the Washington School

Grades 1-3

Grade	N	Pre-Test G.E. Mean	Post-Test G.E. Mean	Average Gain (in Months)
1	102	1.1**	2.4	13
2	74	1.4	3.3	19
3	70	2.2	4.3	21

Grade	Average Gain (in Months) per Month	Average Pre-Test Percentile Mean	Average Post-Test Percentile
1	1.9	*	*
2	2.7	*	*
3	3.0	20	65

* These data not available at the time this table was developed.

** These were twenty-nine students who scored below the lowest level of this test. These students' scores were counted as if they scored at the 1.0 grade level. This inflated the pre-test scores to the level noted and caused the "gain" columns to reflect underestimations of the actual development of students in the first grade.

Table 4 represents the scores of students who took both the pre-test and post-test in the Washington school. The gains were very large at all levels, ranging from an average rate of "growth" of 1.9 months for each of the seven months of instruction between administrations of the achievement test at the first grade level to 2.7 months at the second grade and 3.0 at the third grade level.

At the third grade level, the average student scored at the 20th percentile in October 1977. In May 1978, the average third grader (these are the very same students) scored at the 65th percentile.

It was possible to obtain pre-test and post-test scores of students who were third graders in the Washington school during the 1976-77 year. These students averaged at the 2.6 grade level on the pre-test and 3.8 on the post-test. The interval between pre- and post- testing for this group was ten months, as opposed to seven months for the Barrett-trained students. Using an analysis of covariance (to take differences in pretest scores into account), it was found that the gains in the Barrett group were significantly higher than those of the previous year's third grade group. This, despite the fact that the Barrett students received three months less time of instruction.

While these data do not reflect the results of a controlled study, it is clear that they are consistently positive across all levels studied. The magnitude of these gains are certain to generate interest among professional educators.

Summary of Findings of Standard Measures of Mathematics Achievement in the Cold Spring Harbor and New York City Public Schools

1978-1979

During the 1978-79 school year, Cold Spring Harbor students in grades three, four, and five gained averages of 2.0, 1.3, and 1.9 months in total math respectively for each month of instruction. The test used was the California Test of Basic Skills.

The average student in grades two through five scored higher than 85 percent of his or her peers in total math when compared with a representative national sample. Care must be taken not to view Cold Spring Harbor as exceeding 85 percent of public school districts in total math. In fact, that figure would be substantially more than 85 percent.

Despite declining math scores nationally, this year's third, fourth, and fifth graders scored an average of a half year, nine months, and one full year higher (respectively) on total math than did traditionally taught Cold Spring Harbor students in those same grades three and four years earlier (those years were averaged together for the purpose of this summary).

At all grade levels (three through five), substantially more students scored above the 90th percentile nationally than did traditionally taught Cold Spring Harbor students in 1975.

1979-1980

In February of the 1979-80 school year, the Barrett Method was introduced to teachers within Community School District 3 of the New York City Public School System. Professor Barrett trained teachers of kindergarten and first graders within three schools. He also supplemented the training by having teachers observe demonstration lessons with their classes. The schools involved were Public Schools 113, 165, and 191. Control and experimental classes were formed within each grade.

The training process developed during three months was totally mental. Children did not write anything. The final test administered represented essentially the first time children were asked to translate math concepts into writing.

In the kindergarten classes, students were able to count to 100, add or subtract, mentally, any combination of numbers up to 10, and were able to add, with carrying, combinations up to 20.

The first graders were able to do these aforementioned items, plus recite, with understanding, the 2, 3, and 4 times tables. They were able to add or subtract multi-digit numbers. This process also included carrying.

The gap between the Barrett-trained experimental kindergartners and the control kindergartners was significant. In each of the experimental classes, the greatest concentration of students scored in the 90+ range. In the control classes the greatest concentration of students scored in the 0-49 range.

First graders did significantly well. In a P.S. 191 experimental class, for example, eight students scored over 95% while in the control class, a second grade class in the same school, only five students scored over 95%.

At P.S. 113, ten students in the experimental (first grade) class scored over 91% as compared to only six students who scored over 91% within the third grade control class.

1980-1981

The Barrett Method of Mathematical Instruction was implemented in four Boston City Public Schools during the 1980-81 school year. The four schools were Hennigan, Hale, Guild, and McKay. Kindergarten and first grade teachers were provided with instruction by Barrett in their classrooms as well as in after- school workshops. One second grade teacher also participated in the program, but unofficially.

Evaluating the results of a mathematics program in kindergarten and first grade was very difficult in light of the limited scope of standard tests at these levels. These tests are, at best, insensitive to many of the skills children of this age range are capable of learning but are not traditionally taught. It was decided to use non-standard tests to measure the acquisition of specific skills, many of which are not ordinarily expected of kindergarteners and first graders. First graders averaged 19.2 items correct on the first non-standardized test and 20.7 on the second (see Table 5).

Table 5. Means and Standard Deviations of First Grade Scores on Both Tests

TEST	N	MEAN	STANDARD DEVIATION
Test 1	88	19.2	4.98
Test 2	65	20.7	5.56

1982-1984

In 1984, thirty-four at-risk fifth graders in Bedford-Stuyvesant, Brooklyn, took the New York State Ninth Year Algebra Regents Examination. Sixty-three percent passed with six pupils scoring 90 percent or above.

The percentages below reflect children's growth in mathematics as measured by the New York City Mathematics Test administered in grades 2 through 6 during April 1983.The relatively high 1982 scores in P.S. 24 were the result of previous exposure to Barrett methodology. (See Table 6.)

Table 6. P.S. 44 (District 13)

Grade	1982	1983
2	53%	66%
3	77%	92%
4	58%	75%
5	56%	81%
6	54%	62%
P.S. 207 (District 3)		
2	11%	38%
3	18%	30%
P.S. 144 (District 3)		
2	14%	52%
3	32%	69%

1984-1985

The results of the implementation of the Barrett Method of Mathematics Instruction within two New York City Public School Districts.

Community School District 5, Manhattan, New York

Background

Professor Barrett conducted a project in District 5 during the school year 1984-85. Schools involved were P.S. 30/31, P. S. 154, and P. S. 133.

Results

The overall increase in grade equivalence for the eight fourth grade classes involved averaged out at 1.7.

The greatest increase was in the two "Gates" reading classes with 3.23 and 2.39 for 7G1 and 7G2 respectively. The comparative citywide increase for Gates classes was 1.1 for grade four and 1.3 for grade seven in the 1982-83 school year.

Considering that three of the five grade seven classes were at 2.5 or more grades below grade six in 1982-83, the rise to "within grade equivalence" in 1983-1984 is a marked increase (class 7G1 is at 6.55 grade level from 3.32 and 7G2 is at 5.20 grade level from 2.81).

Community School District 13, Brooklyn, New York

Eighty percent of the pupils at P.S. 44 were on grade level after taking the 1984 New York City Standardized Test in Mathematics. Math scores of this school (consisting of approximately 90% high-risk students) outdistanced students at P.S. 8, Brooklyn, which is located within a high-middle-income area. A fifth grade class of thirty-four students at P.S. 44 took the New York State Ninth Year Algebra Regents examination and achieved a passing rate of 63%. Forty percent of the sixth grade students achieved high school level in mathematics.

Report of the Results of the Barrett Method of Mathematical Instruction within the Atlanta, Georgia, Public Schools

1989-1990

During the 1989-90 school year, the Barrett math program was piloted in selected sections of grades kindergarten through seven in five Atlanta public elementary schools: Campbell, Carter, Hope, Slater, and Pitts.

Teachers received initial and follow-up training in the Barrett math method of instruction. Implementation of instruction was monitored by local school administrators, a staff development coordinator, as well as Professor Barrett.

At the end of the school year, experimental student gain in mean normal curve equivalent (NCE) points was compared with the gain in NCE points for control students. Comparisons were made in three mathematics subtests: computation, concepts, and problem solving. Comparisons were also made in the culminating math exam.

Results indicated that the experimental students outperformed the control students in total mathematics and in all of the mathematics subtests. These differences were highly significant. The performance of the experimental students was also significantly greater than the performance of the control students in mathematical problem solving.

A review of individual school performance revealed that there was a wide range of average student performance within the five schools. However, the average NCE gains for program students at Campbell Elementary School was greater in total mathematics and in all mathematics subtest than were gains by program students at the other four schools.

References

Ausubel, D.P. (1968). *Educational Psychology: A Cognitive View*. New York: Holt, Rinehart & Winston.

Barrett, E. (1979). *Personal Discovery: A Pedagogy for Mathematical Competence*. New York: The Barrett Learning Dynamics Corporation.

---. (1989). *Teaching through Context: Finding the Bridges Which Make Learning Inevitable*. Unpublished manuscript.

---. (1990). *Teaching Mathematics through Context*. Available from Professor Everard Barrett, P.O. Box 409, N. Baldwin, NY 11510.

Battig, W.F. (1968). "Paired-Associate Learning." In T. R. Dixon and D. L. Horton eds., *Verbal Behavior and General Behavior Theory*. Englewood Cliffs: Prentice-Hall.

Bruner, J. (1963). *The Process of Education*. Boston: Harvard University Press.

Carey, S. (1977). "The Child as Word Learner." In M. Halle, J. Bresnan, and G. A. Miller, eds., *Linguistic Theory and Psychological Reality*. Cambridge, MA: MIT Press.

Garner, W. R. (1966). "To Perceive Is to Know." *American Psychologist* 21:11-19.

Piaget, J. (1970). *Genetic Epistemology*. New York: Columbia University Press.

Rohwer, W. D., Jr., and Levin, J. R. (1968). "Action, Meaning and Stimulus Selection in Paired-Associate Learning." *Journal of Verbal Learning and Verbal Behavior* 7:137-41.

Stolzberg, M. (1977). *Evaluation of Barrett Educational Science Techniques in the Roosevelt Public Schools*. Roosevelt, NY. Unpublished study.

---. (1979). *Analysis of Results of Standard Measures of Mathematics Achievement in the Cold Spring Harbor Public Schools (Grades Two through Five)*. Unpublished study.

---. (1981). *An Informal Evaluation of the Barrett Method of Mathematics Instruction in Four Boston Schools Using Non-Standard Tests*. Unpublished study.

Vaidya, S. and Chansky, N. (1980). "Cognitive Development and Cognitive Style as Factors in Mathematics Achievement." *Journal of Educational Psychology* 73: 326-30.

4. Other Current Programs and Strategies That Work in Teaching Mathematics and Science to At-Risk Youth

Randolf Tobias

Science Skills Center

The Science Skills Center, located in Brooklyn, New York, has demonstrated for well over ten years that it can improve science skills of at-risk students. Beginning in 1979, a group of African American scientists and teachers joined together to volunteer their professional expertise to children living in the Brooklyn community. In forming the Science Skills Center, these professionals sought to open the world of science to approximately 100 children and to act as role models who would inspire the next generation of African Americans toward careers in science and technology.

The center's curriculum offers a wide variety of scientific enrichment programs that include robotics, biology, chemistry, physical science, computer science, rocketry, geology, oceanography, botany, and algebra. The center receives major state and municipal funding as well as grants from the private sector.

A four-tier program for children ranging from ages seven to fifteen is offered. The Saturday program involves children engaging in ongoing hands-on science projects that they are committed to continue from session to session. A weekly after-school program combines lectures and laboratory work so that students may pursue in-depth scientific studies. Since the center is based within a public school, there is also an "early bird" program for students who attend the school. This program begins every morning at 7:45 a.m. and is available throughout the day for the use of the school's classes. In addition to programs conducted during the school year, the center offers a six-week summer science institute where students explore many facets of science.

Teaching Strategies

The center implicitly and explicitly instills in its students who are predominantly African American that science is not difficult. Students quickly realize that to study science is to study the natural order and evolution of the earth's elements, their relationship to one another, and their broader relationship to the universe. Students also learn that scientific knowledge is based upon the operation of general laws obtained and tested through a fundamental scientific method. As a result of this type of teaching (broken down to the appropriate intellectual level of students), science becomes demystified and student fears become arrested.

The Center's director, Michael A. Johnson, is a thermo-dynamics engineer who believes that students should have scientific hands-on experiences. The natural curiosity of these students is massaged, and they become excited about learning. Many of the students are individually mentored through specific projects. It is not unusual to see these young students employing microscopes or bunsen burners, or checking over a human skeleton or skull. Students dissect frogs, and they learn about the similarities between the brain of a cow and a human being. The center's facility is small but decorated with an array of scientific charts, pictures, and models. Tables are arranged in a circular fashion with up-to-date electronic microscopes on each table.

In the summer of 1989, the Science Skills Center, in cooperation with the State University of New York Health Science Center, conducted a special course for junior and senior high school students that served as an introduction to scientific research and medical careers. This experience allowed students to rotate through several areas of research and medical specialties at the university. Courses were taught by the university faculty and graduate students. Highlights of the program included, viewing dissections in human anatomy, observing open heart surgery, studying the problems in pediatric aids, learning molecular biological research techniques, participating in a class in medical ethics, and learning the steps in performing a physical examination.

The center also employs field trips as a vital part of their teaching strategy. During the 1989 school year for example, thirty-five elementary school students, ranging from ages nine through twelve, visited the State University of New York. The students engaged in a discussion about AIDS, after which they were led to cell culture laboratories in the Basic Science Building. The students were able to learn about cells and view cultures through the electronic microscope. They were also taken to the nursing center where they received first-hand information about transplant surgery. Before concluding their visit of the campus, the youngsters were advised about medical careers.

Program Assessment

In 1989, students in the fourth through eighth grades scored high on science and mathematics examinations given by the New York State Department of Regents. These regents examinations covered tenth year biology and ninth year mathematics. The highest mathematics score (96) was made by a fifth grade student and the highest biology score (96) was made by an eighth grade student. (See Table 1 and Table 2)

**Table 1. Science Skills Center
1990 Regents Exam Scores
Sequential 1 Math**

STUDENT AGE	GRADE LEVEL	REGENTS GRADE	CLASS GRADE
10	5th	96	95
12	7th	92	90
11	6th	92	90
12	7th	87	85
11	7th	85	85
12	6th	84	80

**Table 2. Science Skills Center
1990 Regents Exam Scores
Biology**

STUDENT AGE	GRADE LEVEL	REGENTS GRADE	CLASS GRADE
13	8th	96	95
12	7th	95	95
13	8th	95	90
9	4th	88	90
12	8th	88	85
11	7th	88	85
11	7th	88	80
14	8th	85	85
13	8th	84	80
11	6th	82	80
13	8th	80	85
10	5th	77	85
11	6th	77	70
10	5th	71	70
11	6th	69	70
13	8th	68	70

Table 3. Science Skills Center
1990 Advance Placement Grade
Biology

STUDENT AGE	GRADE LEVEL	REGENTS GRADE	CLASS GRADE
13	8th	82	90
11	6th	73	80
13	8th	78	80
12	8th	70	85
11	7th	83	75
11	6th	66	75
12	7th	68	80
13	8th	72	70
11	6th	72	75
12	7th	85	95
13	8th	71	90

A 1990 Evaluation of the Science Skills Center Summer Program: Building Access to Science Enrichment (BASE)

These data suggested that:

1. The summer program had a positive effect on most students' ability to skillfully maintain a formal journal of what they had learned and experienced.

2. The summer program had a positive effect on enhancing the career aspirations of most students.

3. The summer program had a positive effect on generating the continuing commitment of faculty participation.

4. The summer program significantly influenced the career choice confidence level of almost every student participating.

5. When the program began, slightly more than 70 per-
    cent of the students were almost certain of a career in
    the health and science profession. When the program
    ended, almost 90 percent of the students were abso-
    lutely certain about a career in the health and science
    profession.

6. The faculty held a favorable opinion about the sum-
    mer program, which had a positive impact on the
    students as they endeavored to choose a career in the
    health and science profession. (Turner, 1990)

Computer Assisted Learning

Computer Assisted Learning (CAL) also located in Brooklyn, New York, is the first hi-tech learning center of its type in
the Bedford-Stuyvesant community. The center uses computers to teach basic academic skills and computer literacy. Dr.
Martha Hennington, President of CAL, states that "The use of
computers causes students, particularly those at risk, to exhibit an intense interest in learning and exhibit an extraordinary effort in mastering a subject. It is common knowledge
that by the year 2000--less than sixteen years from now--the
literacy criterion, in addition to the three R's, will be a knowledge of computers."

Dr. Hennington has trained and consulted thousands of
business and educational professionals in using computers
effectively. She has taught elementary through graduate
school, and she is presently on the faculty of the City University of New York consulting with school districts and universities concerning computer usage.

The program for students consists of mathematics and
reading tutorials and computer literacy and summer school
programs. Specific courses include Introduction to Computers,
Programming for Beginning Children, Word Processing, Computer for Families, Computer Concepts for Young People,
Lotus 1-2-3, dBASE III, and Computer Assisted Preparation
for specialized tests, e.g., GED, PSAT and SAT.

Since 1983 some 450 students elementary through high school age have taken courses at CAL.

Teaching Strategies

Students are first given diagnostic tests in reading and mathematics. A skills profile sheet is then developed and an individual learning approach designed. CAL offers mini-workshops for school groups that make field trip visits to its site. In addition, CAL also offers specialized programs for school administrators, teachers, parents, and other interested adults.

The Computer Summer Camp is one of CAL's highlights and of particular interest to parents and children during the summer recess. Open to children from ages seven through fifteen (at a remarkable low tuition), these youngsters receive an enriched program consisting of computer instruction, basic academic skills, and career-awareness seminars. Lunch and recreational activities are also added to heighten student motivation.

The Computer Assisted Learning facility provides an open, nonthreatening environment where small-group instruction and accelerated learning take place. The facility provides hardware and software equipment and materials, so plenty of hands-on experiences can take place. Educational games in mathematics, science, reading, and computer proficiency are used to further enhance the children's learning experience. Computer-related field trips are also a vital part of the center's teaching approach.

Program Assessment

In general, Dr. Hennington has observed a noticeable improvement in the academic performance of her students within their respective schools. Mathematics and reading standardized test scores have risen, entire attitudes toward learning have become positive, and student self-image has vastly improved.

Table 4. Computer Assisted Learning Center

GRADE	ENTRY-TEST MATH	ENTRY-TEST READING	RE-TEST MATH	RE-TEST READING
6th grade student	5.7	—	9.0	—
7th grade student	4.4	—	6.6	—
7th grade student	3.2	—	4.1	—
7th grade student	4.6	5.9	5.3	5.9
8th grade student	7.0	—	7.8	—
4th grade student	3.4	2.7	3.4	3.1

Entry-level tests revealed that some of the junior high school students scored at an elementary school level. After enrolling in CAL's after-school program with one-to-one computer assistance, these students (over a six-week period) improved by at least one grade level.

Table 5. Computer Assisted Learning Center

GRADE	ENTRY-TEST MATH	RE-TEST	ENTRY-TEST READING	RE-TEST
7th grade student	4.4	10.0	5.4	6.0
7th grade student	7.8	9.0	10.0	10.0
7th grade student	6.3	6.9	5.9	7.4
8th grade student	7.8	8.9	5.2	7.6
5th grade student	6.0	7.0	6.1	6.1

After attending CAL's summer computer camp program, these students continued on in a two-week tutorial for reading and math.

Institute for Independent Education

The Institute for Independent Education, Inc., located in Washington, D.C., was established in 1984. The institute provides technical assistance to independent neighborhood and community schools in the areas of in-service teacher training and curriculum and proposal development. There are an estimated 211 such schools throughout the United States. IIE also assists education policymakers, scholars, parents, and others by clarifying national and international issues affecting the independent sector of American education.

The institute focuses primarily on independent elementary and secondary schools that are located in America's inner cities, usually operated by and for African Americans, Hispanic Americans, Asian Americans and Native Americans. Most of these groups are at risk with respect to academic accomplishment within the public school system.

Dr. Joan Davis Ratteray, the institute's founder and president, states that among the significant services provided by the institute are the unique in-service mathematic seminars for teachers. As early as 1986 twenty-seven math teachers and administrators from these independent schools attended a twelve-day seminar entitled "Math Alive!" These teachers and administrators journeyed from California, Louisiana, Mississippi, Georgia, North Carolina, Pennsylvania, Washington, D.C., New Jersey, and New York.

Teaching Training Strategies

IIE Math Seminars provide the following training:

- Computer immersion in the subject content of numbers theory, number systems, probability, statistics, and geometry

- Problem-solving sessions in each of the content areas

- Classroom management strategies in relation to mathematics and science

- Specific teaching strategies in the content areas

- Computer-assisted instruction in the content areas

Other opportunities afforded seminar participants are "Informal Learning Teams" where teachers are given opportunities to share teaching strategies. "Networking Groups" are formed which give teachers a chance to sustain their professional development when they return to their respective schools. Lectures are also presented from nationally known specialists in the areas of mathematics, information systems, learning theory, and multicultural education. These lectures concentrate on classroom application from recent research.

Program Assessment

The 1986 "Math Alive Seminar" funded by the National Science Foundation resulted in the publication of two teacher training tests: "Teaching Mathematics: Culture, Motivation, History, and Classroom Management, Volume I;" and "Teaching Mathematics: Bridging the Gap between Philosophical Perspectives and Mathematical Principles, Volume II."

IIE completed a major study in 1987 which resulted in the publication of "Dare to Choose: Parental Choices at Independent Neighborhood Schools." A second research project began that year, initiating library and archival research into the history of independent schools.

Successful IIE programs from 1988 until the present include updating the data base of "Dare to Choose," a directory of independent schools, publication of a "primer" on how to start and maintain an independent school, and securing donated material from the Library of Congress. These materials consisted of 2,000 new and used books (reference, protocol, fiction for children) and audio visuals. IIE has also published a variety of other informational literature on the value of an independent neighborhood education.

Family Intervention

Lightfoot (1978) published a study on the relationship between families and schools. The study, appropriately titled *Worlds Apart,* established that since the culture, perceptions, and expectations of families and schools are different, there is a natural and expected conflict between these institutions. Her findings brought to light that educators, social scientists, and policymakers distort and misrepresent the true nature of the family-school relationship.

Although the study was conducted within the elementary grades, Lightfoot's conclusions addressed family-school relationships within secondary schools. A finding of significant importance to parents or guardians of black adolescents is that, although many of the interactional dimensions between families and schools remain constant across grade levels, different issues emerge as children grow older, become more independent of their families, become more identified with the values and perspectives of their peers, and feel less need for parental protection, guidance, and support. Lightfoot also discusses the ritual and contrivance of Parent-Teacher Association meetings and the fact that parents usually ask for a conference with teachers when they sense their children are unhappy with the school environment or are not learning to read.

Thirteen years have past since the advent of the Lightfoot Study, and since 1978 more educators and public school systems have come to understand the importance of families and schools as partners. This concept is especially key with respect to increasing at-risk student proficiency in mathematics and science. Parent participation for example is key to Brooklyn's Science Skill Center's philosophy of involving the entire family in the child's education. Courses for parents include a class on "Mathematic Phobia." Parents are also counseled on how to support children in their scientific studies. Comer (1988) points out that "schools must win the support of parents and learn to respond flexibly and creatively to students' needs." A significant portion of his intervention project at Yale University's Child Study Center is building supportive bonds that draw together children, parents, and school. This concept came about because of Comer's own personal childhood experience and his hunch that the failure to bridge the social gap between home and school may lie at the root of the poor academic performance of at-risk children. This hunch, however, was also rooted in

> the fact that a child develops a strong emotional bond to competent caretakers (usually parents) that enables them to help the child develop. Many kinds of development in social, psychological, emotional, moral linguistic and cognitive areas are critical to future academic learning. The attitudes, values and behavior of the family and its social network strongly affect such development. (Comer, 1988)

Comer's intervention program within two schools in New Haven, Connecticut produced significant results. Fourth graders from both schools (from 1964-84) for example made steady gains in mathematics. The Iowa Test of Basic Skills was used as the measuring instrument. Average percentile gains on California Achievement Test scores (particularly in mathematics) from 1958-87 were larger for ten mainly black schools in Prince Georges County, Maryland, that used the Comer program than they were for the school district as a whole (Comer, 1988). This success has been duplicated at more than fifty schools around the country.

"Family Math," a project developed by the EQUALS program at the Lawrence Hall of Science, University of California, Berkeley, established classes that help parents and children learn to enjoy doing mathematics together. Parents and children attending Family Math classes learn problem-solving skills and build an understanding of mathematics with hands-on material. These classes are held weekly for an hour or two for approximately two months. Teachers, parents, retired people, and community workers teach within these programs. Two-day workshops are offered at the Lawrence Hall of Science and at selected sites for educators who desire to facilitate Family Math courses in their own schools and communities. Centers are now established in Arizona, New Mexico, Indiana, and Oregon.

"Family Science" is another program with similar goals and activities as Family Math, by involving parents with their children's science education. One of the major goals of Family Science is to show how science is already a part of everyday life and how important it is for future job opportunities. All activities are hands-on and use ordinary household items like measuring cups, spoons, empty paper rolls, and rubber bands as sources for learning science. Currently, the program is being piloted at seventy-five sites across the nation for kindergarten through eighth grade students and their families. Family Science is based at Northwest EQUALS, Portland, Oregon.

Communications Arts Within Mathematics and Science

Clear communication between teacher and students, students and other students, and students and their families is fundamental to math and science comprehension—and within this era of "high tech," communication between student and computer must be added (a strategy stressed at the Computer-Assisted Learning Center). How many statements have we heard for example that "this particular brand of software is user friendly," or that "peer-mediated techniques served to make subject matter more understandable for students." These statements refer to different communicative approaches and patterns that present information in new and different ways, thus making the learning process palatable.

Communication arts within math and science is of particular importance to Barrett's discussion of teaching mathematics through context. This strategy does have the potential of "unleashing the power of the contextual learner," a must for the at-risk student.

The research of Sheila Hollander lends additional strength to this view. From 1977 until the present, Hollander has conducted research on specific areas of the contextual approach in an effort to shed light on greater mathematical proficiency among students. The results of an early study entitled "The Effect of Questioning on the Solution of Verbal

Arithmetic Problems" (1977) discussed a very important communicative teaching skills, the ability of teachers to break a verbal math problem down into its component parts and make distinctions between its correct and incorrect aspects. Students should also be asked to explain their rationale for the process used in solving the problem. Hollander points out, additionally, that students are rarely asked questions about their problem-solving behavior—and rarely is there a distinction made between an error in comprehension of mathematical relationships and one of computation.

> Teachers should provide opportunity for regular discussions of the rationale behind the correct solutions of a problem. These discussions may be held either before a problem is attempted or subsequent to its completion. It is to be expected that all students, not just the individual reporting on his own rationale, should benefit from these explanations which serve to facilitate the student's organization of knowledge. It appeared that questioning encouraged the students in this study to reconsider their behaviors and to refer again to the test in order to supply answers. Therefore, the teacher might experiment with techniques requiring students to review the facts presented within a problem and the relationship of these facts to each other rather than merely to review the computation employed. Questioning and discussion appear to be basic and profitable techniques worthy of regular employment within the elementary classroom. A technique resulting in a 40 percent improvement in altered responses is worthy of additional investigation.

Hollander's 1988 article entitled "Teaching Learning Disabled Students to Read Mathematics" is directly germane to the at-risk population, since 88% of this population is one to three years below grade expectancy in computation (Koppitz, 1971). The article identified certain features of writing which are characteristic of mathematics textbooks and workbooks and indicated how these materials may cause disabled students difficulty. Hollander's conclusions are as follows:

Mathematics textbooks and workbooks are among the most difficult of the content area reading materials. These materials have many characteristics which differentiate them from narrative material. All students, but particularly those who are learning disabled, must receive specific instruction in recognizing and accommodating to these differences. The teacher must understand that "reading requires language comprehension, semantic processing, unique types of language behavior, and reorganization of schemata stored in memory" (Zintz and Maggart, 1984, xv). Strategies to accomplish these learnings are not acquired incidentally. There must be a shift in instructional emphasis from rote decoding and computation drill to analysis of the language conveying the concepts of each verbal arithmetic problem.

The teacher of the learning disabled must help them develop metacognitive techniques to deal with the reflective and associative aspects of math reading material as well as the vocabulary and symbols which are specific to this content area. Mathematical concepts are embedded within an intertwined verbal and symbolic format with which many students, including those not learning disabled, often encounter difficulty. The increase in the number of states requiring minimum competence testing in math (McCarthy, 1980) indicates the necessity for a look at the reasons for failure that go beyond computation. The emphasis on this process has characterized remedial efforts to the virtual exclusion of a study of the characteristics of the language of instruction without which there can be no comprehension.

Hollander's 1990 publication entitled "Oral Reading Accuracy and Ability to Solve Arithmetic Word Problems" is too detailed to elaborate upon here. (See reference section for chapter citation.) She does, however, provide guidelines that mathematics teachers might find helpful when assisting their students to read, understand, and solve arithmetic word problems. Some of these guidelines for teachers are as follows:

1. Students should actively be helped to develop awareness of the necessity for either total or partial reread-

ing and, if necessary, rewording of verbal arithmetic problems until each problem becomes comprehensible at a level with which the reader feels comfortable.

2. As the technique described above is employed, and students read orally and provide their interpretation of the material, the teacher might ask, "Did that make sense to you?" and require an explanation of the portion read as it relates to the whole.

3. Listening to the student's oral reading and rereading will help the mathematics teacher learn if the student is distracted by irrelevant data or confused by technical symbols.

4. Rewording sometimes introduces error unrecognized by the reader. Rather than merely asking for the correction, the teacher should seek this recognition from the other students and question why and how the student's restatement has undermined comprehension.

Conclusion

Discussing current programs and strategies as presented in this chapter brings to light specific strategies that are recommended to successfully teach mathematics and science to at-risk youth. These strategies are:

1. *Providing pre-service and in-service teaching training* geared for the educationally at-risk population. (See chapter 2, "'You're Teaching Mathematics!' In-service and Pre-service Preparation in Mathematics and Science," and the Institute for Independent Education within this chapter.)

2. Instilling within the minds of children that *math and science are not difficult to master,* and that there is no mystery about these subjects whatsoever. Teachers must also state that math and science are not re-

served for the brightest children, and that all children can consider a career in these areas.

3. *Showing relationships between math and science and the everyday lives of children,* e.g., setting up group activities where mathematics is used in purchasing or trading items and mixing elements within a "demonstration kitchen" to create baked or cooked goods. (See other strategies under "Teaching Strategies," in this chapter.)

4. *Use diagnostic approaches.* Teachers should employ pre-testing so that they can ascertain strengths and weaknesses of students. Prescribed teaching strategies designed to strengthen weak skills and enrich strong skills should follow. A post-test should be administered toward the end of the strategy in order to assess the quality and quantity of student improvement. This approach has particular importance in the enhancement of math skills.

5. *Provide hands-on materials and equipment as often as possible.* This strategy is of particular importance in teaching major aspects of the natural sciences, i.e., biology, chemistry, and energy. These subjects should not be taught solely from textbooks. Examples of hands-on materials and equipment in the natural science area are microscopes, specimens, energy cells, bunsen burners, personal computers, aquariums, house plants, and educational games.

6. *Small-group or one-to-one instruction* has proven beneficial, especially when students need to proceed at their own pace. This type of teaching affords students opportunity to ask questions otherwise not posed in large groups. Teachers are also afforded the opportunity to employ other materials, e.g., programmed instructionals, modules or computer-assisted strategies. In some teaching situations one-to-one instruction is called student mentoring.

7. *Helping students to achieve mastery in specific skill areas of mathematics and science.* Within this process the teacher first defines what specific objectives students are expected to learn. Materials and activities are then selected and organized around these objectives. Summative assessments are developed for each set of objectives to be mastered. Mastery approaches are recommended for at-risk students since math and science objectives are broken down into manageable sequential units. At the end of each sequential unit, a formative assessment of student learning behavior is carried out. The teacher specifies a score or a performance standard of mastery, which is equivalent to students mastering 80% to 90% of the material. If mastery is not accomplished, alternative approaches and materials are developed.

8. *Proactive tutoring* is a tutoring strategy employed while the class is in session, rather than the traditional after-school reactive model. The current strategy allows students to receive tutoring on the spot as the lesson is being taught. In addition, both the tutor and tutee have the benefit of using the same materials used by the rest of the class. The proactive model also addresses specific problem areas as defined by the student and teacher. Tutoring in this regard is in shorter sequels, thus allowing students to quickly return to the "main stream." Tutors can be teacher aides or peers. Teachers themselves can become tutors, provided that they are facilitating small groups rather than teaching the entire class.

9. Family Intervention Strategies—see "Family Intervention" in this chapter.

10. Communication arts—see "Communication Arts within Mathematics and Science" in this chapter. See also, chapter three, "Teaching Mathematics through

Context: Unleashing the Power of the Contextual Learner."

11. *Field trips* that will enhance units of instruction within mathematics and science are very important for three reasons:

   a. Visits to specific sites can provide quality learning experiences for students, making the environment external to the school a classroom. Information and materials gathered from the field can be brought back to the school classroom for analysis, thus converting the school classroom to a laboratory of learning.

   b. Field trips enable students to see firsthand applications of what is taught in the school. These experiences reinforce the relationship between math and science and the daily lives of children.

   c. Exposing students to quality field experiences may motivate them into thinking about a career in mathematics, science, or related fields.

The positive assessment data provided within this chapter should encourage educators to employ and adapt as many as these programs and strategies as possible within their own environments. These approaches can open up other avenues of success for youth at risk.

References

Burns, Marilyn. (1986). "Does Math Make Good Homework?" *The Instruction* (September): 97.

Comer, James P. (1988). "Educating Poor Minority Children." *Scientific American* 259(S):42-48.

Hendler, Marjorie R. (1990). *Studying Science, Math, and Technology: A Parents Guide to Programs, Places, and Publications.* Center for Advanced Study in Education, The Graduate School and University Center of The City University of New York, 1-3.

Hennington, M. (1991) Computer Assisted Learning, Inc., Brooklyn, New York, Interview, July 19, 1991.

Hollander, Sheila K. (1977). "The Effect of Questioning on the Solution of Verbal Arithmetic Problems." *School Science and Mathematics*, 77:659-61.

---. (1988). "Teaching Learning Disabled Students to Read Mathematics." *School Science and Mathematics* 88 (6):509-15.

---. (1990). "Oral Reading Accuracy and Ability to Solve Arithmetic Word Problems." *School Science and Mathematics*, 90 (i):23-27.

Institute for Independent Education. (1986). American Choices: A Report of the Institute for Independent Education, Inc. 2 (2):1-4.

---. (1986-87). Annual Report: 1-8.

Koppitz, E.M. (1971). *Children with Learning Disabilities: A Five-Year Follow-up Study.* New York: Grune and Stratton.

Lightfoot, S. L. (1978). *Worlds Apart: Relationships Between Families and Schools.* New York: Basic Books.

McCarthy, M. (1980). "Minimum Competency Testing and Handicapped Students." *Exceptional Children*, 47 (3):166-73.

New Youth Connections. (1989). "Math and Science, Who Needs It?" *News Magazine*: 8-13.

Nuhty, Peter. (1989). "The Hot Demand for New Scientist." *Fortune*, (July): 155-58.

Ratteray, Joan D. (1991). Institute for Independent Education, Washington, DC, Interview, September 4, 1991.

Ratteray, Oswald M. T. (1986). *Teaching Mathematics Volume I: Culture,* Motivation, History and Classroom Management. Washington, DC: Institute for Independent Education.

Science Skills Center, Inc. (1990). Eighth Annual "Minds in Motion Program: 2

State University of New York, Health Science Center at Brooklyn."

"SUNY Brooklyn Invests in the Future of Gifted Youngsters." *Focus* VIII6.

Stenmark, Jean Kerr, et al. (1986). *Family Math.* Berkeley: Lawrence Hall of Science, University of California, Berkeley.

Turner, Thomas M. (1990). *An Evaluation of the Science Skills Center Summer Program* (BASE).

Zintz, M.V., and Z.R. Maggart. (1984). *The Reading Process: The Teacher and the Learner.* Dubuque, IA: William C. Brown.

5. Raising Student Self-Esteem through Mathematics and Science

Randolf Tobias

There are two requisites prior to initiating any teaching strategy in raising at-risk students' self-esteem through mathematics and science:

1. Bringing students to a level of first believing in themselves;

2. Then building upon this level in such a way that will convince students that they can succeed.

Stephen Chinlund of the Episcopal Mission Society, in cooperation with the self- esteem work of Thomas Turner, has put into operation within the public schools of New York City a structured program designed to build self-esteem, community, and responsibility among at-risk youth. The program entitled "Network in the Schools," started in 1989, affirms and concentrates on the strengths and gifts of young people rather than focusing only on their problems. "Network in the Schools" in fact accomplishes the two aforementioned requisites. These requisites are accomplished through the use of a four-part series of round circle discussions. In each series of discussions (which are held in a classroom for one period a week), a facilitator skillfully asks students questions designed to stimulate impromptu discussion of opinions, ideas, and sometimes innermost feelings. Each series of discussions contributes toward strengthening self-esteem from different perspectives.

The first part of the four part series motivates each student to make "self-affirming statements," e.g., "I am William Anderson. I intend to become a scientist so that I can find a cure for cancer." This process breaks the taboo against immodesty. Children need places where they can celebrate their successes. Many children cannot do that at home. As a result, they disbelieve the truth that they are valuable human beings. The second part engages youngsters in expressing their social concerns. Through this process many students have expressed their concerns and outrage about deplorable social conditions that surround their lives, e.g., substance abuse, health hazards, crime. This is also a time that youngsters can share their stress, pain, anger, and frustration, an important part of being fully human. Students are then asked during the third part of the series to develop a short-range doable plan-- an objective that can be realistically reached. This particular level is significant for three reasons: (1) making a plan can provide a healthy sense of power and control, (2) each individual plan has been created by the student and not the facilitator or teacher, and (3) these plans can be within the cognitive domain which includes the fulfillment of such objectives as homework and classwork, or the affective domain which includes social objectives, e.g., better cooperation with one another in school and at home or helping the school to become a better environment in which to learn.

Finally, in *Part Four*, there is a short period of silence. For those young people who are exposed to a continuous din of television, sirens, music, earphones, arguing, and other noise, silence can be frightening because it is unfamiliar. In experiencing Part Four, it is possible for young people to learn that silence can be a friend. With some guidance about breathing and simple meditations, they can learn to be at peace in silence, eventually welcoming it rather than fearing it or running from it.

The time of silence is also intended to be a counterbalance to what may be experienced as a certain willfulness in the first three parts. The cumulative experience of the first three parts of the meeting can sometimes lead to a kind of overhead "rush" or feeling of power, which is as unrealistic as the powerless feeling that the meeting is intended to correct. So the silence is a time of yielding; especially, yielding to the recognition that there is much over which we will never have control--such as the feelings of other people, accidents, the caprice of certain diseases, and the separation of physical death.

The cumulative effect of many Four-Part meetings, over weeks and months, is a strong new sense of self-control, empowerment, self-esteem, and a widening field of responsibility and the possible. (Chinlund, 1991, 10)

The round circle strategy enables all students and the facilitator to face one another and even held hands (whenever appropriate), evoking a sense of family.

Since its inception at the beginning of the 1989-90 school year, "Network in the Schools" has been established or introduced in more than ten elementary and junior high schools. It is active in eight New York City schools in four boroughs and has reached more than 500 students, teachers, and parents. It has developed a reputation as a positive influence within schools, affecting not only students (its primary target), but also faculty and parents (Chinlund, 1991). Network staff members continue to meet with school staff, parents, and students until they feel confident to run their own meetings. Network staff also continue to be available as consultants.

The final stage of implementation for the individual school occurs when there are sufficient administrators, school staff, and students trained in Network meetings and other processes to allow incorporation of the program as an ongoing part of the life of the school.

Using the Network Model or one similar as a base, student self-confidence and self-esteem can be strengthened through creative mathematics and science teaching strategies. These strategies fall into four broad areas:

1. Demystifying mathematics and science;

2. Showing relationships of math and science to every-day student experiences: practical considerations;

3. Teaching mathematics and science from an integrated perspective; and

4. Ethnocentric approaches to teaching mathematics and science.

Demystifying Mathematics and Science

Teachers must implicitly and explicitly instill within the minds of at-risk learners that mathematics and science are not difficult subjects to master. This particular objective can be accomplished by providing students with as many opportunities as possible to succeed in computation, problem solving, and comprehension within a structured environment. The terms "opportunities to succeed" and "structured environment" are significant. With respect to the latter term, Bruner (1960) argued that "good teaching that emphasizes the structure of a subject is probably even more valuable for the less able student than for the gifted one, for it is the former rather than the latter who is most easily thrown off the track by poor teaching." Structure would also include:

- Selection or development of appropriate materials that can be understood by students

- Plenty of teaching reinforcement

- Constant monitoring and evaluation of student progress

- Length of time spent on an aspect of problem solving

- Constant practice and repetition experiences for students in the use of the four fundamental computational operations—adding, subtracting, multiplication, and division

The reader is urged to read the conclusion of chapter four as it relates to achieving mastery in specific skill areas of mathematics and science. The mastery approach speaks to the former term "opportunities to succeed." Since mathematics and science (particularly mathematics) are developmental, the subject matter should be presented to at-risk youngsters in progressive steps. As each step is mastered, there is a kind of built-in reward of accomplishment for the student. Self-confidence is also strengthened during this process. Even though each step becomes a little more challenging, teachers must remind students that they are slowly building upon their mastery of former steps and, as a result, their math and/or science skills are becoming stronger.

Constant monitoring and evaluation of students' progress within this type of a structured environment will get students used to the idea of being evaluated. Using a criterion-referenced approach, that is to say "an assessment of students' strengths and weaknesses," rather than the traditional testing approach, which may suggest that "the kid is a failure," reduces test anxiety. Building in opportunities for self- and peer-evaluation strategies are also helpful in reducing anxiety and simultaneously raising self-esteem.

Also, the fear and mystery of an area such as technology can be dispelled through an understanding of what technology really is. Technology represents the emergence of a "super tool," which is in actuality the extension of our hands and fingers. These tools enable us to complete given tasks easily and quickly. Though the complexity of today's technological world cannot be minimized, machines represent vast developmental improvements upon sticks, ropes, and wheels that were primarily used for hunting, defending, gathering, farming, moving, and building. Teachers can tell youngsters that the evolution of math, science, and technology is based upon other peoples ideas and that there is always room for improving ideas as long as the fundamental premises are understood and mastered.

The most up-to-date technological system in use today to assist children in losing their fear of mathematics is the personal computer. Approximately fourteen years ago, my son (who was then twelve years of age) came home from school with a pocket calculator. I became concerned later on in the evening as he proceeded to do his mathematics homework with the aid of this miniature machine. As a teacher/educator, I had taken some philosophical positions about the impact of educational technology upon the field of education, particularly the science of teaching. One of these positions was "that the computer should not rob children of using their brains to critically think and to solve problems." I guess he was reading my mind, for before I could open my mouth he said "don't worry Dad, I'm just checking my answer with this calculator— that's all." From that particular evening until the present, I have supported the position that computer-assisted instruction (CAI) is good. The key word here is *assist*. If computers could act as extensions of teachers to enhance learning, then I would support the concept.

What has happened over the past twenty-six years with computers and education is just phenomenal. From the teaching standpoint, the computer has enhanced both teaching strategies and skills. From the learning standpoint, the computer has fostered retention, application, critical thinking, and problem solving. With respect to mathematics, a multiplicity of CAI software has been developed. Division, fractions, algebraic equations—you name it—the software probably exists.

There are many combinations and permutations of CAI. Programmed Instructional Software is the most popular. These "friendly" reinforcement programs allow individual students to work at their own pace. Self-evaluative features are built in to allow students to correct their own work. Drill and practice programs, for example, are designed to reinforce learned skills, and they actually provide immediate feedback on the correctness of responses. This is exactly what at-risk students of mathematics need. The formats of many math drill and practice programs are often visually appealing. They include educational games that increase student motivation and participation. Many drill and practice CAI software packages can also serve as tutorials.

With respect to science, demonstration CAI programs can graphically illustrate concepts that would be otherwise impossible, or at least very difficult to see: anything from planetary motion, to the flow of blood through the heart, to a bloodless dissection of a frog!

What Is Computer Assisted Instruction?

CAI involves the use of the computer for direct contact with the learner. In this capacity, the computer can be used for practicing recently acquired skills. It can also be used to teach new skills (Hofmeister, 1984). The process of CAI not only reinforces and introduces new skills, it assists in the diagnosis of pupils' strengths and weaknesses. This process, in addition, can help monitor pupils' learning progress. Though the computer has the capacity to create shortcuts for the learner, CAI if used correctly can actually sharpen thinking and problem-solving skills. Using the computer to create shortcuts would be detrimental to the learning process.

B. F. Skinner stands foremost in his analysis of student/machine relationships and consequently programmed instruction. In his research, Skinner was concerned with problems surrounding stimulus-response and learned behaviors. Skinner additionally was quite thorough in underscoring important features of teaching machines: "To my mind, the most important feature is that the machine in question should be programmed so as to enable the student to pass through a carefully designed sequence of steps, often of considerable length. Each step must be so small that it can always be taken, yet in taking it, the student moves somewhat closer to fully competent behavior. The machine must make sure that these steps are taken in a carefully prescribed order" (Skinner, 1969). This inductive notion was supported a few years earlier by Jerome Bruner (*Process of Education*) within the context of how instruction is best delivered. More importantly, the inductive step-by-step approach is key to successful CAI software programs as they relate to teaching at-risk youth.

Showing Relationships of Math and Science to Everyday Student Experiences: Practical Considerations

Willoughby (1990) makes the following statement:

> Most people who find themselves in a situation that requires mathematics either don't recognize that good decisions depend on mathematical thought or don't make the best decisions because they are unable or unwilling to think mathematically. The fast-food clerk who returns $98.16 change to a customer who puts down a ten dollar bill, the young mother who believes she's certain to have a girl next time because she's had three boys already ("these things even out in the long run"), and the person who believes that a 40 percent chance of rain on Saturday and a 60 percent chance of rain on Sunday, guarantee a 100 percent chance of rain on the weekend are all examples of people failing to think mathematically when they should. (1)

Children live math and science every day of their lives but may not realize it. If teachers could incorporate this idea in their teaching, students would be more apt to draw concrete relationships between the world of the school and the world of their practical lives.

Mathematics can be linked to real-life experiences of all children. For very young children that reality usually is something physical such as ice cream sticks, fingers, chairs, people, distance walked, heights of friends and relatives, and so on (Willoughby, 1990). For older students the reality may be the natural or social sciences, puzzles, or even some part of mathematics itself (Willoughby, 1990). Real-life experiences as they relate to learning science are even more apparent. The kitchen where elements are mixed for baking, frying, boiling, and broiling contains at least 100 or more practical illustrations of the science of chemistry. The issues of health and nutrition as they relate to the lives of at-risk youngsters help to make science come alive. Good health is a requisite to educational success; therefore, an excellent unit of study in biology could include these issues.

A discussion with students about the variety of sources from which proteins, vitamins, and minerals can be obtained beyond red meats, pork, and starches is scientifically relevant. Because of the high cost of food in inner-city areas, practical information about comparative shopping, nourishing foods, and other methods of food preparation would be relevant.

With the advent of substance abuse, the HIV virus, AIDS, and the increase of venereal disease among our nation's youth, science (if taught creatively) can be used to motivate students to consider a career in the health/science professions. They could conceivably see the pursuit of a science career as a moral and ethical mandate for them to become a positive influence in their communities.

What about the student's world of electronics and energy? Let us look at this incomplete list of scientific items that constantly surround children:

VCRs	Stereos	Car Horns
Computer Games	Car Engines	Doorbells
Telephones	Heating and Air Conditioning Systems	Watches
Television	Refrigerators	Clocks

Not only can imaginative lessons emerge from these topics, but perhaps future physicists, electronic engineers, electricians, technicians, and energy and environmental specialists.

Children talk, use, refer to, and are involved in mathematics every day of their lives but fail to recognize their involvement. Children use mathematical data for example when they are discussing basketball. The height of a "center"; average "buckets" from the free-throw line; and average points scored in a game are all mathematical discussions. Time on a clock; scores made within a card game; and the use of dice all involve mathematics. Even rhythmic musical patterns can be discussed mathematically. In the light of these examples, teachers can approach discussions concerning averages, percentages, fractions, estimations, probabilities, and so on with new and creative vigor. Shopping at supermarkets and malls can yield new techniques for teaching addition, subtraction, division, multiplication, and other elementary math skills. Various mathematical games can teach business math skills such as buying, selling, borrowing, taxes, and interest rates. Projects that involve building toy models can yield new approaches to the teaching of geometric principles involving lines, circles, angles, and distance.

There is enough raw material housed within everyday events of children to develop several mathematical linkages between the school and the real world of the child.

Teaching Mathematics and Science from an Integrated Perspective

Integrated approaches toward teaching mathematics and science should be a serious consideration as a means of heightening the global thinking skills of at-risk youngsters. The compartmentalized approach within public schools still remain virtually unchanged. Integrated approaches encourage students to see relationships between different subject matter and simultaneously curtail isolated patterns of thinking.

The following model represents a possible integrated approach to teaching health as an aspect of science. This model is actually a part of larger model entitled "Humanistic Concerns of the Upcoming Century: Problems and Process" presented at the Sixth Triennial Conference of the World Council for Curriculum and Instruction, Noordwijkerhout, The Netherlands (Tobias, 1989). It is an example of the range of possibilities that schools and teachers can use in engaging at-risk students in integrated learning approaches.

A World Health Curriculum Model Integrating Science, Social Studies, Literature and Music

Rationale

Robbins and Freeman (1988) report that over the past twenty-five years the United Nations, through the World Health Organization has had significant success in the global immunization programs that it sponsors. These programs totally eradicated smallpox a decade ago and more recently have significantly reduced annual death and disability caused by polio and tuberculosis. Yet new or improved vaccines are still needed for the many other infectious diseases that cause unnecessary death and disability in the developing world. Children are the prime target of vaccination programs, because they are the chief victims of infectious diseases. In Africa, Asia, and Latin America, pneumonia, malaria, meningitis, and typhoid fever kill an estimated 14 million children younger than five every year. It is not a lack of scientific know-how that is impeding the development of the needed vaccines. The obstacles to testing, mass production, and distribution of the needed vaccines are economic and political. The UN is not equipped to produce the vaccines, and the handful of manufacturers that have the technological skill to do so have little interest in the task.

The estimate of worldwide HIV infection at the end of 1988 was 300,000. The World Health Organization estimates that the world total of AIDS cases over the next four years will be anywhere from 500,000 to three million (Samuels, Mann and Koup 1988). As Jon Tinker, president of the Panos Institute, observes: "The global underclass, those who live in rural and urban shantytowns, who cannot afford condoms and are not reached by family planning advice, who cannot read and therefore are least likely to be reached by educational campaigns, who have little or no access to health clinics, who may have to sell their own blood to buy food—this global underclass will likely bear a disproportionate share of AIDS' misery" (Heise, 1988).

Besides the limitations of the WHO immunization program and the spread of the HIV virus, there are other world health concerns that must be confronted in the classroom. In the United States, for example, children are beginning alcohol use at about 12.5 years of age. The average American who does not have a drug habit will pay between $850 and $1,000 in 1989 to test drug and alcohol abuse problems (Kumpfer, 1987). Much of this money will be collected through taxes and spent by police or state agencies. Insurance companies and health care providers will collect another portion (Hansen, 1988). Researchers estimate that 84 percent of the deaths from lung cancer could be avoided if individuals never started smoking (Totten, 1988), and intervention assistance teams in schools can prevent teenage suicide by identifying signs of emotional distress and destructive behaviors long before adolescence (Seibel and Murray, 1988).

Possible Teacher-Student Activities

World Health

1. Arrange a site visit to a research institute or clinic where emphasis is placed on researching causes and preventions of major diseases, e.g., cancer, AIDS, heart diseases. Questions, answers, and distribution of pertinent literature would occur at the site.

2. Develop a debate on a health related controversial issue, e.g., tobacco industry verses the non-smoking contingency, or the treatment of mental illness. Novels and plays written around the theme of mental health and biographies of musicians who fell ill to substance abuse would be integrated along with student research assignments.

3. Invite agencies devoted to physical fitness to address students in the areas of nutrition and exercise.

4. A sample culminating project: Involve students in a campaign designed to inform the immediate commu-

nity about preventive health care. This activity would involve designing a video presentation, a school-based preventive health care resource center, oral student presentations, and computer printouts. Actual dissemination of information would occur via school-based community meetings and distribution of literature to parents and community residents. A possible fund-raising activity to enhance the project would be a musical concert given by teachers and students. Formative and summative evaluative procedures would be integral parts of the activity.

Ethnocentric Approaches to Teaching Mathematics and Science

From the standpoint of valuing cultural diversity, the educationally at risk should understand that their ethnic group made original contributions to the fields of mathematics and science. This process essentially accomplishes three things: (1) it gives children a sense of ownership of the knowledge base, (2) it enable children to feel a sense of pride in knowing that members of their cultural group contributed to an important field, and (3) "since members of my cultural group have done it, maybe I can also."

Ethnocentric approaches to teaching mathematics and science can be accomplished in three ways:

1. Identifying the geographical region that particular aspects of math and science had its roots;

2. Identifying specific personalities associated with math and science accomplishments; and

3. Use illustrations of ethnic contribution via guest speakers, field trips, and visuals.

Two Illustrations

1. In teaching a lesson on the Pythagorean Theorem in 1975, Professor Everard Barrett used three ethnic

groups in his development. These groups were Greek, African, and Italian. He first presented a historical account of Pythagoras, a Greek born on the island of Samos about 584 BC. Barrett then pointed out that Pythagoras studied philosophy under Tales in Greece and later went to Egypt to study geometry. While in Egypt, Pythagoras observed the pillars of the temples and their shadows and consequently became interested in the right triangle and the relationship of their sides. Barrett finally explained that when Pythagoras became a teacher of philosophy and mathematics in Crotona, southern Italy, he organized a society of Italian scholars known as the Order of Pythagoreans. This society contributed much to the progress of geometry and also in the study of numbers.

2. In a team-taught science class developed at the Brooklyn Street Academy during the early 1980s, teachers Emery Williamson and Edwin Griffith presented a model lesson consisting of a discussion and demonstration of the human circulatory system. Using a plastic facsimile of the human circulatory system, the class was engaged in learning about the following aspects:

    A. Heart (valves)
    B. Blood Vessel
        1. Artery
        2. Vein
        3. Capillary
    C. Blood
        1. Red Blood Cells
        2. White Blood Cells
        3. Platelets
        4. Plasma

Special emphasis was placed on two African American doctors who did outstanding work relating to the circulatory system. These doctors were Charles Drew, whose pioneering work led to the development of blood plasma, and Daniel Hale Williams, who performed the world's first open heart surgery. Visuals of these personalities were also presented to the students.

These sample lessons can serve as examples of many other types of ethonocentric approaches that can be introduced to students. More importantly, these approaches contribute toward building positive self-images. Ethnocentric approaches enable the experience of all cultures to become the focal point of knowledge. They do not discount, for example, Asiatic, European, African, or Native American contributions, but they do discount Eurocentric claims (directly or through implication) that Greece was the beginning of Western civilization, if not all civilizations.

All ethnic groups have contributed fundamental knowledge bases that as a result created standards which significantly affected large-scale populations throughout the world—standards within philosophy and theology; logistics and ethical constructs; engineering and architecture; mathematics and science.

Conclusion

In discussing raising student self-esteem through mathematics and science, consideration was first given to general requisites in self-esteem building. A discussion of the Episcopal Mission Society model (Chinlund/Turner) illustrated how this task could be accomplished. Building on this model, the chapter focused on four discrete mathematics and science teaching strategies that strengthen self-esteem.

This presentation, however, does not discount other strategies that are also important in building student self-confidence and self-esteem. Some of these strategies are as follows:

1. Involve students with the physical experience of using concrete materials in learning and applying math and science principles. Both materials and activities should be instructionally innovative, so that students can begin to make sense of these fields (particularly mathematics).

2. Encourage students to work cooperatively in groups as well as individually. Cooperative learning groups are seen as vehicles for a new sort of instructional discourse in which students would do much more of the teaching. Students would learn from their own efforts to articulate and explain ideas, and they would learn from their mates' ideas. (Cohen, 1991, 23)

3. Allow students to openly express there ideas and interpretations of math and science materials from which they are working. These open discussions enable students to feel that their statements are important and perhaps valid in the way they read, see, and interpret ideas.

References

Barrett, Everard. (1985). *The Pythagorean Theorem.* A lesson plan.

Brunen, Jerome S. (1960). *The Process Of Education.* New York: Vintage Books.

Chinlund, Stephen J. (1991). *Network in the Schools: An Introduction.* A pamphlet. New York: The Episcopal Mission Society.

Cohen, David K. (Fall, 1991). "Revolution in One Classroom. American Federation of Teachers." *American Educator*: 16-48.

Hansen, William B. (1988). "Effective School-based Approaches to Drug Abuse Prevention." *Educational Leadership* 45 (6):9.

Heise, Lori. (January-February, 1988). "Aids: New Threat to the Third World," *World Watch*: 21.

Hofmesiter, Alan. (1984). *Microcomputer Application in the Classroom.* New York: CBS College Publishing.

Kumpfer, K. (July, 1987). "Current Drug Education Programs in the State." Presentation at The National Conference of State Legislators, Indianapolis, IN.

Robbins, Anthony, and Phyllis Freeman. (November, 1988). "Obstacles to Developing Vaccines for the Third World," *Scientific American* 259 (5): 126.

Samuels, Michael E., Jonathan Mann, and C. Everett Koop. (1988). "Containing the Spread of HIV Infection: A World Health Priority," *Public Health Reports* 103 (3): 221.

Siebel, Maxine, and Joseph N. Murray. (1988). "Early Prevention of Adolescent Suicide," *Educational Leadership* 45 (6):49.

Skinner, B. F. (1969). "Teaching Machines," *Educational Technology: Basic Readings*, Albert B. Miller, ed. New York: Simon and Schuster.

Tobias, Randolf. (1989). "Humanistic Concerns of the Upcoming Century: Problems and Process." Paper presented at the Sixth Triennial Conference of the World Council for Curriculum and Instruction, Noordwijkerhout, The Netherlands.

Totten, S. (1988). "The Myriad Dangers of Tobacco Use: Ignorance Is Anything But Bliss," *Educational Leadership* 45 (6):30.

Williamson, Emery, and Griffith, Edwin. (Circa, 1980). *A Lesson Plan of the Human Circulatory System.*

Willoughby, Stephen S. (1990). *Mathematics Education for a Changing World.* Alexandria, VA: Association for Supervision and Curriculum Development, 1.

6. Mathematical Competence and the Educationally At Risk Learner: Implications for Assessment

Eleanor Armour-Thomas

Once again the plight of educationally at risk students in U.S. schools is receiving serious attention from researchers, practitioners, and policymakers alike. The growing concern about the educationally at risk learner, particularly as it relates to mathematics and science, is fueled partly by demographic projections and shifts in the nation's economic base and partly by changing conceptions of what it means to be an educated person in the twenty-first century. According to recent trends (noted by Oakes, 1990, for example), workers of tomorrow will comprise large proportions of non-Asian ethnic minorities, particularly those from African and Hispanic backgrounds—groups that historically have not pursued careers in mathematics and science. But, these are the very areas from which the continued growth in our economy will depend and from which a high level of cognitive competence will be expected from its workers. As some researchers have argued, in a technologically oriented economy, workers would be needed at all levels who can exercise good judgment and decision making (Resnick, 1987; Zuboff, 1988). Given these demographic and economic projections our educational system will need to develop and nurture mathematics and science competence in all our students, including those who currently fit the profile of the educationally at risk learner. But demographic and economic considerations are not the only rationale for enabling competence in our children. There is a moral and ethical imperative as well. Commitment to the dual ideals of equity and social justice requires that educational resources should be equitably distributed on the basis of need. Educationally at risk learners, in terms of what we know about them academically, are in need of educational services to better prepare them to participate as informed, capable, and productive members of our democratic society. In terms of mathematics, if we are to develop and nuture competence in the educationally at risk learner there are a number of issues that require attention: the standards in mathematics toward which they should aspire; a knowledge base regarding the factors that influence mathematical performance; an understanding of the strengths and weaknesses of the educationally at risk learner in terms of this knowledge base; assessment procedures that are sensitive to the identification of strengths and weaknesses; curricula and pedagogical interventions that are adaptive to these identified needs.

This chapter begins with an examination of the concept of the educationally at risk learner. Next the standards for mathematics, developed by the National Council for Teachers of Mathematics, are presented to indicate the mathematical competencies expected of the educationally at risk learner. Following this, a review is conducted on the extant knowledge base with respect to factors influencing mathematical performance with a view toward a consideration of how such information might be used to better understand the areas of strengths and weaknesses of the educationally at risk learner. The next section explores the implications of this knowledge base for assessment. The chapter ends with recommendations for educational policymakers and classroom teachers with respect to assessment issues.

The Educationally At Risk Learner

In the literature the label "educationally at risk" is often-times used interchangeably with the term "educationally dis-advantaged" to describe a subset of the student population whose status characteristics include low socioeconomic standing in the social order, membership in ethnic/racial minorities, and living in a single-parent family (Durken, 1981; Pallas, Natriello, and McDill; Peng and Takai, 1983; Rumberger, 1987; Schreiber, 1979). In terms of functional characteristics or attributes that describe the behavior and attitudes of the individual, the educationally at risk learner is portrayed as having negative attitudes toward school and a history of truancy and misconduct (Kagan, 1990). But perhaps the most common and negative functional characteristic associated with the educationally at-risk learner is significantly low academic performance as measured by standardized achievement or aptitude tests.

In an earlier research, the Coleman report (1966), based on a national sample, revealed that black students on the average scored one standard deviation below that of white students on different nationally normed standardized achievement tests. More recently, results from the National Assessment of Educational Progress (1985) indicated that the reading and writing skills of black and Hispanic students are substantially below that of white children at each of grades 3, 7, and 11. The pattern of less than adequate academic performance for racial/ethnic minorities is also evident in the dropout rate. Ekstrom et al. (1986) reported that black and Hispanic youths are less likely to complete high school than white youths. Using the yardstick of academic achievement and aptitude, it would appear that low or inadequate performance on tests is a defining attribute of the educationally at risk learner. Any attempts, therefore, to improve the academic performance of this subpopulation would, in part, require that we identify correlates of academic performance that are essentially cognitive in nature.

NCTM Standards

In 1989, the National Council of Teachers of Mathematics (NCTM) developed its *Curriculum and Evaluation Standards for School Mathematics*. The document calls for the development of mathematical literacy and power of all North American students, K-12. The kinds of mathematical competencies required for the attainment of mathematical literacy and power include the following:

- Conceptual and procedural understanding of number, operations, geometry, measurement, statistics, probability, functions, and algebra

- Inventing, conjecturing, problem solving, and reasoning

- Connecting mathematical concepts, principles, and their applications within mathematics and between mathematics and other intellectual activites

- Communicating mathematically

- Using a variety of methods to solve nonroutine problems

- Having an appreciation of the beauty and value of mathematics

- Self-confidence and a disposition to seek, appraise, and use spatial and quantitative information to make decisions and solve problems

The vision of mathematical literacy and power is inclusive of the educationally at risk learner as well, as is evidenced in a recent statement (April, 1990) by the NCTM Board of Directors. According to members of the Board,

> By "every child" we mean specifically—students who have been denied access in any way to educational opportunities as well as those who have not; students who are African American, Hispanic, American Indian, and other minorities as well as those who are considered to be a part of the majority; students who are female as well as those who are

male; and students who have not been successful in schools and in mathematics as well as those who have been successful.

The NCTM sent a clear message to the educational community about the kinds of competencies toward which their initiatives in assessment, curriculum and pedagogy should be directed. However, some educators might legitimately claim that they have little informed knowledge about strengths and weaknesses of the educationally at risk learner in mathematics. In the absence of such a knowledge base, it would be difficult to plan and implement nurturing experiences that most likely would lead to the development of the kinds of competencies enunciated in the NCTM's *Curriculum and Evaluation Standards for School Mathematics* . In the section that follows I review the research in cognitive psychology and mathematics education with a view toward a more informed understanding of the factors that influence mathematical performance.

Factors Influencing Mathematical Performance

Over the past two decades, a great deal of theoretical and empirical work in cognitive psychology and mathematics has been conducted among proficient and less proficient learners, experts and novices, for the purpose of identifying factors that function to facilitate or impede performance. Among the more promising variables investigated include the following:

- Metacognitive knowledge and skills
- Prior knowledge and knowledge structures
- Misconceptions
- Inert knowledge
- Socio-cultural context

Metacognitive Knowledge and Skills

Metacognitive knowledge and skills describe the awareness and use of executive mental operations individuals use to control and regulate their own thinking. In the educational and psychological literature, these capabilities are used interchangeably with constructs such as "higher-order thinking" (Baker, 1991; California State Department of Education, 1989; Resnick, 1987) or "metacognition" (Brown, 1978; Flavell, 1976; Ghantala, 1986; Sternberg, 1986). Although perspectives differ in emphasis, there is common agreement that metacognitive thinking occurs in three broad phases over the course of any given cognitive enterprise: *planning* (processes selected prior to any problem-solving action); *monitoring* (processes selected to keep track of what has been done, what is currently being done, and what still needs to be done for problem solution); *evaluating* (processes selected to judge the outcome of any action against criteria of effectiveness and efficiency).

Work in the area of mathematical problem solving suggests that the deployment of metacognitive skills underlie successful performance. Shoenfeld (1987) found that expert mathematicians engaged in decision-making and management behaviors at critical junctures during the problem-solving process. In contrast, novice problem solvers did not appear to use these metacognitive processes and often found themselves lost in the pursuits of "wild geese." More recently, Artzt and Armour-Thomas (in press), in their investigation of the analysis of problem solving in small groups, found that a continuous interplay of cognitive and metacognitive behaviors was necessary for successful problem solving. Other reviews of studies of mathematical problem solving (e.g., Garofalo and Lester, 1985; Silver, 1987) suggest that a fundamental source of weakness underlying children's performance may lie in students' inabilities to actively monitor and subsequently regulate the cognitive processes used during problem solution.

There is also some evidence about the role of metacognitive knowledge—the ability to bring knowledge about thinking to consciousness and reflection—in successful mathematical performance. For example, Peterson and her colleagues (Peterson and Swing, 1982; Peterson et al., 1982;

Peterson et al., 1984) found that students' general metacognitive knowledge for classroom learning was significantly related to student achievement. Using a stimulated-recall procedure, students were asked to recall their thoughts during mathematics instruction. Students reported that they were able to judge their own understanding, to diagnose and monitor their understanding and specific cognitive processes such as reworking problems, applying information at a specific level, checking their answers against an external criterion, etc.

Prior Knowledge and Knowledge Structures

Knowledge may be defined as the accumulation of concepts, ideas, rules, strategies, procedures, and principles within a specific domain that an individual acquires over time. In short, it denotes the contents of one's past experiences. However, possession of sheer quantity of knowledge is a necessary though not sufficient condition for doing well on any complex task of interest. Units of knowledge are organized in an interrelated way and stored in memory as knowledge structures commonly referred to in the literature as schemata. There are a number of characteristics or properties of knowledge structures that can facilitate or impede learning. For example, Anderson (1984) claims that knowledge structures have active attributes that enable the individual to be reflective, planful, and to make inferences. Glaser (1987) contends that the degree of elaborativeness and differentiation of knowledge structures allows individuals to perceive meaningful patterns in memory which enable them to form representations of problems that lead to meaningful action. Gagne and Dick (1983) suggest that knowledge structures help retention of new material by providing a scaffold or framework for storage but may also modify the new information by making it "fit" the expectations of already existing knowledge structures.

In accounting for the relationship between knowledge structures and learning and performance, researchers have categorized them into three groups. Knowledge structures

that consist of the organization and differentiation of concepts, principles, formulas, rules, ideas, etc., are referred to as
declarative knowledge. Knowledge structures that consist
of the organization and differentiation of procedures and
strategies, heuristics, and algorithms are referred to as *procedural knowledge.* And finally, knowledge structures that are
organized and differentiated in a manner that enables individuals to make decisions and judgments regarding when or why
declarative and/or procedural knowledge should be used are
referred to as *conditional knowledge.*

Carpenter (1985) provides an interesting scenario of how
the model learner uses different kinds of knowledge in a learning situation. According to Carpenter, the learner brings to
the problem-solving situation knowledge about various types
of problems and mathematical content and a repertoire of
possible solutions. He or she reads the problem of interest to
be solved. This process activates knowledge of various dimensions about the problem alluded to earlier that is then used to
generate hypotheses about problem-solving procedures or
even predictions or estimates of potential solutions. As the
problem-solving process continues, the learner makes decisions regarding problem representation, conceptually or
graphically. Next, the learner compares this information to
earlier hypotheses and makes revisions if necesary. As the
learner solves parts of the problem or realizes that hypotheses
are not working, he or she returns to the beginning of the
problem-solving process to reconsider strategies, set subgoals,
or even redefine the problem.

Within the last decade, numerous studies have been conducted with regard to the role of prior knowledge and knowledge structures in performance of complex mathematics tasks.
Investigations of students solving problems in high school algebra have found that proficient learners quickly perceive the
semantic structure of problems, classify them into problem
types (e.g., a triangle problem, a ratio problem), and recognize
the principles or theorems associated with each problem type.
The way such problems are perceived allow them to form

representations that trigger appropriate problem-solving procedures and solutions in memory.

Other studies that analyzed the performance of experts and novices on a variety of tasks in mathematics provide evidence for the critical role of deep understanding of principles underlying computational skill (Resnick, 1982, 1984) and principles underlying children's numerical reasoning and counting skills (Gelman and Gallistel, 1978; Greeno, Riley, and Gelman, 1984).

Misconceptions

Misconceptions may be described as distorted knowledge that results when new information is filtered through knowledge structures that are themselves superficial, naive, incomplete, or even downright incorrect. It may be recalled that a basic function of knowledge structures is that they provide a context for meaningful interpretation of new information so that individuals think about new information in terms of what they already know. Consequently, to the extent that existing knowledge structures are not well developed and poorly differentiated and organized, individuals' thinking will reflect serious misconceptions.

There is a great deal of evidence of misconceptions in mathematical research. For example, Davis and McKnight (1980) found misconceptions among third or fourth graders in subtraction problems. In a problem such as 7,002 − 25, a typical incorrect answer was 5,087 indicating a misconception about the process of borrowing. Brown and Burton (1978) two years earlier had found similar evidence of systematic error in subtraction among children. At the high school level, Martz (1980) described four misconceptions from a list of thirty-three such errors in algebra:

- Evaluating xy when x equals −3 and y equals −5 as −8
- Evaluating 4x when x equals 6 as 46 or 46 x

- Claiming that an individual cannot multiply by x because "you don't know what x is"

- Calculating 2x divided by 2x to be 0.

Inert Knowledge

Whitehead (1929) described knowledge as inert when it is accessed only within a limited number of contexts although it has applicability across multiple domains. Over the last fifteen years, several studies have provided evidence of this problem in unskilled or novice learners. For example, Gick and Holyoak (1980) found that students who just learned information for the solution of a problem were unable to spontaneously use it to solve an analogous problem unless they were explicitly prompted to do so. Similiarly, Bransford and his associates conducted a number of experiments that showed that academically unsuccessful students unlike their successful counterparts were unable to recognize and use helpful information in activating previously acquired knowledge structures for successful task performance (Bransford et al., 1981, 1986).

Socio-cultural Context

In recent years there is converging evidence from a variety of disciplines to suggest that thinking is situated within the environmental context in which it develops and is applied (Bronfenbrenner, 1979; Brown, 1989; Gardner and Rogoff, 1982 and Wertsch, 1979). Many years earlier, a noted anthropologist, Clifford Geertz, recognizing the inseparability of context and cognition, stated:

> the human brain is thoroughly dependent upon cultural resources for its very operation; and those resources are, consequently, not adjuncts to but constituents of mental activity (Geertz, 1962, 730)

Similarly, Ceci (1988) argues that contextual influences play an important role at two points in the development of cognitive competence: in the initial crystallization of cognitive potentials and in the later activation of fully developed cognitive potentials at the time of its measurement. With regard to the initial crystallization of cognitive potentials, Ceci contends that different developmental contexts are perhaps differentially important for the development of different cognitive potentials. For example, a setting in which children are encouraged to read and play word games may facilitate the development of verbal reasoning more so than a setting in which other types of cognitive potentials are supported or nurtured. Conversely, an environment with little or no contextually relevant stimuli may impede or constrain the development of cognitive potentials.

Several studies in mathematics have documented how the acquisition, understanding, and application of mathematical concepts and principles grew out of individuals' sociocultural experiences. For example, Lave and her associates (1984) investigated the relationship between subjects' cognitive abilities on real-world tasks and on traditional measures of cognitive competence. Their findings showed that subjects were able to use arithmetic operations remarkably well while shopping in the supermarket. However, when these same competencies were assessed on a formal mental arithmetic test, no relationship was found between performance on that test and subjects' shopping performance. In a similar naturalistic observation study Scribner (1984) found that experienced dairy factory workers demonstrated remarkable judgment and skill in filling milk orders in the most economical manner. Again, such proficiency was unrelated to the dairy factory workers' performance on various high school test scores (e.g., grades, IQ, arithmetic test scores). In yet another study of candy selling and math learning among Brazilian children, Saxe (1988) found that sellers with little or no schooling displayed complex mathematical skills in their out-of-school activities that contrasted sharply with mathematical skills learned in school.

In accounting for these contextually-related effects on mathematical performance, D'Ambrosio (1985) had an interesting perspective. He used the term "ethnomathematics" to describe the intuitions and informal procedures for dealing with mathematical phenomena that children bring to school—intuitions and informal procedures developed and applied within their own sociocultural experiences.

Toward an Interactive Model of Mathematical Competence

Both theoretical and empirical research are supportive of the notion that mathematical competence is, in part, a function of the possession and application of metacognitive knowledge and skills over the course of a mathematical enterprise of interest. But the possession of mathematical concepts and principles as well as the degree of organization, differentiation, and elaboration of such concepts and principles into mathematical knowledge structures work in dynamic interaction with metacognitive knowledge and skills. Furthermore, to the extent that the sociocultural context plays a socialization role in shaping the development and application of metacognitive knowledge and skills as well as the development and application of mathematical knowledge and knowledge structures, the nature and quality of the performance will reflect such a sociocultural reality. If the mathematical experiences toward which children are exposed are rich and are embedded within a nurturing sociocultural context, then individuals will develop mathematical competence. If, on the other hand, mathematical experiences are poor or inadequate and are enmeshed in a hostile or unnurturing sociocultural context, then, predictably, mathematical competence will not emerge.

How might these theoretical and empirical research studies about the factors influencing mathematical performance and the attendant conceptualization of mathematical competence inform our understanding of the problem of the educationally at risk learner? To recap, it has become increasingly evident that the sociocultural context can positively or negatively influence the acquisition, understanding, and application of mathematical competencies. Also, a review of the literature suggests that the possession of metacognitive knowledge and skills, the possession of a body of well-construed mathematical knowledge and fully differentiated, well-organized, and elaborated knowledge structures, influences mathematical performance.

In applying these understandings to the educationally at risk learner, it is quite plausible that weaknesses in some or all of these correlates of mathematics performance contribute to their less than adequate academic performance on standardized tests. However, this analysis does not assume that the educationally at risk learner has no strengths in these areas. Indeed, I would suggest that inappropriate or insufficient attention to the cognitive strengths of the educationally at risk learner in his or her out-of-school experiences may have contributed to the problem. If educators are serious about mounting initiatives for improving the academic performance of children so labeled, then, to begin, our assessment procedures must be able to identify strengths and weaknesses of the educationally at risk learner in terms of those correlates of mathematical performance. The next section considers the properties or characteristics assessment procedures must embody if they are to yield accurate, detailed, and complete information of the strengths and weaknesses of the educationally at risk learner.

Implications for Assessment

Assessment Criteria

As the research has evidenced, mathematical performance is the product of a number of interdependent factors that work in dynamic interaction with each other. Metacognitive knowledge and skills are used to activate relevant concepts and principles which are themselves structured in memory in an organized and differentiated manner. Furthermore, the context in which these competencies are developed and nurtured influence when and how they are deployed in the service of performing any complex task of interest. In applying these understandings to mathematical performance, it would seem plausible that our assessment procedures must correspondingly be comprehensive and multifaceted if they are to yield the kinds of information that would be useful for prescriptive educational planning and intervention. Listed below are criteria that in the author's judgment may be used to judge the validity of assessment procedures in mathematics:

1. *Multiple Methods.* Metacognitive knowledge and skills in mathematics as well as domain-specific knowledge and knowledge structures in mathematics are related but different competencies; therefore, more than one type of assessment procedure is required. Procedures should allow for the assessment of both thinking and content skills.

2. *Different Modalities.* Individuals perceive and represent information differently; therefore, assessment procedures must allow for the identification of strengths and weaknesses in knowledge and skills through modalities that include but are not limited to spatial, iconic, verbal, and concrete representations.

3. *Multiple formats.* Since metacognitive knowledge and skills as well as the nature and quality of one's knowledge and knowledge structures depend on the kinds of experiences to which one is exposed, then assessment procedures should allow for the expression of thinking and content skills that reflect different experiential histories. Furthermore, procedures should allow for more than one correct answer since individuals differ not only in their perceptions of the problem but in their solutions as well.

4. *Authentic tasks.* Tasks selected for assessment must be non-trivial and non-routine. These tasks should allow for the elicitation of the nature and quality of metacognitive knowledge and skills in mathematics in addition to mathematical knowledge and knowledge structures.

5. *Authentic experiences.* Children acquire knowledge and skills and attitudes from sociocultural experiences both in and out of school. Assessment procedures should elicit real-world metacognitive knowledge and skills in mathematics as well as real-world knowledge and knowledge structures in mathematics. In addition, assessment procedures should also assess these competencies from in-school experiences.

Recommendations for Educational Policymakers

The above-mentioned criteria are not evidenced in the assessment practices we currently use to appraise mathematical competence. Indeed, current standardized tests are inappropriate for the identification of strengths and weaknesses of the educationally at risk learner in metacognitive knowledge and skills or the nature and quality of mathematical knowledge and knowledge structures. If, however, educators are to be guided by the vision of mathematical competence espoused by the NCTM's *Curriculum and Evaluation Standards for School Mathematics* and the findings from research regarding mathematical performance, then their policy decisions and practices must reflect a commitment for change. If these decisions are made at a policy level, then classroom teachers would be empowered to use assessment practices that are truly in the service of instruction of the educationally at risk learner. The following propositions, though not exhaustive, are recommended at the school level and are therefore addressed to principals, assistant principals, and teachers who are involved in educational decision making.

- Reflect a commitment to the NCTM standards in the vision and mission statement of the school's educational plan

- Reflect a commitment to assessment procedures that would yield diagnostic information regarding strengths and weaknesses in mathematical performance

- Acknowledge the integrity of in- and out-of-school experiences in mathematics
- Provide staff development opportunities in alternatives to standardized tests
- Provide an atmosphere that is supportive of classroom teachers' use of alternatives to standardized tests
- Allow teachers to use data yielded from alternatives to standardized tests to plan curricula and pedagogical initiatives
- Allow teachers to align mathematical content and pedagogical strategies with the data from alternatives to standardized tests

Recommendations for Classroom Teachers

If classroom teachers are to provide learning experiences for the nurturance of mathematical competence in the educationally at risk learner, they must rely on assessment procedures that identify strengths and weaknesses underlying mathematics performance at a sufficient level of detail. Information at this level of detail can be used to target interventions according to identified strengths and weaknesses in mathematics. In this section, the author describes a category of assessment generically referred to as "performance assessments" that teachers may find useful in gathering evidence of students' mathematical competence.

Performance Assessments

Performance assessments are measures that use direct judgments and appraisal of student behavior. They include solution to complex problems, exhibitions, projects, investigations, portfolios of work accumulated over time. For each type of performance, individual or groups of students are required to actively solve problems, to generate solutions, to construct responses and create products. Such procedures enable teachers to gather information about what students actually know and can do, the process of their thinking as well as the product of their thoughts. Furthermore, they offer students the opportunity to bring to the classroom knowledge and skills acquired in their out-of-school experiences and to apply their classroom knowledge and skills to their real-world experiences. There are a variety of approaches that can be used to collect data on student performance and include the following: observations, open-ended questions, structured interviews, written problem-solving assignments, computer-assisted assessment systems, portfolios, and student reports and self-inventories. Each will be examined in turn.

Observations. Observations are techniques used to gather a variety of information regarding student competencies while they are actually solving a problem. For example, observations of children working in small groups allow the teacher to hear students' comments and questions about the task of interest. Such comments and questions provide clues to the teacher with regard to the use of metacognitive strategies in problem solving such as planning, problem representation, monitoring, and evaluation. Comments and questions can reveal students misconceptions, the nature and quality of their mathematical knowledge, and knowledge structures.

Open-ended questions. Open-ended questions provide tremendous choice to students in demonstrating their knowledge and skills. Such procedures allow students to explain or justify their responses, to use idiosyncratic strategies to solve problems, or to select information from a variety of experiences to support their responses. Such information enables the teacher to gain insights about the nature and quality of students' conceptual understanding, the nature and quality of their thinking, and the nature and quality of their knowledge and knowledge structures.

Structured interviews. Structured interviews provide a rich source of data on one or two students at a time regarding their thought processes, their understandings of concepts and principles, and their attitudes and beliefs toward mathematics. Structured interviews differ from observations in that the task of interest and the types of questions and probes are determined some time before. Structured-interview data can be gathered through audio- or videotaping devices for more detailed analysis later.

Written problem-solving assignments. Written problem-solving assignments focus on the quality of mathematical knowledge, understanding, and thinking strategies that students employ over the course of the problem-solving task rather than the product or the answer obtained. Although such assignments allow for the identification of correct or incorrect answers, they serve the purpose of diagnosing systematic errors or misconceptions about mathematical concepts and principles. Also, written assignments allow the teacher to focus on the assessment of whether students considered all the options in a problem situation, whether they represented the information in the problem in a manner most likely to lead to problem solution, and whether they selected the appropriate strategy for problem solving.

Computer-assisted assessment systems. Computer-assisted assessment systems allow for the assessment of the nature and quality of students' knowledge structures as well as their metacognitive skills. In such a system the computer generates items to elicit student responses about particular dimensions of conceptual understanding and thought processes regarding a complex word problem. For example, some items may require students to define or label mathematical concepts; other items may require students to infer relationships between concepts; yet other items may require students to select a modality to represent information in the problem from an array of modalities or even select a strategy from a list of possible procedures. In this manner, the teacher gathers qualitatively rich information regarding students' weaknesses in problem solving.

Portfolios. A portfolio is a container that showcases the student's past knowledge, understanding, and skills as well as his or her beliefs and attitudes toward the subject matter of interest. A wide variety of items may be collected by the student over time as evidence of the student's competencies. The teacher makes judgments about the quality of the performance of the student's work. In terms of evidence of mathematics competence, the student can show knowledge and conceptual understanding of mathematics and the kinds of metacognitive knowledge and skills he or she used in problem-solving tasks. It is ideally suited for providing choice to the student for demonstrating mathematical competence in real-world and classroom contexts.

Student reports and self-inventories. Student reports and self-inventories provide retrospective information about students' thoughts, their perceptions, beliefs, and attitudes about their experiences in a subject. In gathering such information from self-reports, the teacher provides a structure for allowing students to respond to specific mathematical concepts and principles or components of the problem-solving process. Self-inventories provide similar information as reports with slight variation. Usually, the teacher provides a list of items that assess students' self-knowledge of their own metacognitive knowledge and strategies. Students respond by checking items that apply or rate the degree to which items reflect their own judgment of their knowledge and skills. In some instances, items seek to assess students' feelings, attitudes, and beliefs about mathematical concepts, principles, or problems.

Techniques for Scoring Performance Data

So far, the discussion has focused on methods of collecting data on a variety of issues associated with student performance—their knowledge, understanding, and skills in addition to their perceptions, attitudes, and beliefs about the subject matter. This section addresses techniques that teachers may use to score such varied data. Among the more commonly used techniques are checklists and rating scales and analytic and general impression scoring.

Checklists and Rating Scales

Each technique consists of a list of items about various aspects of students' behavior. Checklists allow the teacher to record the presence or absence of behavior, whereas rating scales enable the teacher to judge the quality of the behavior in question. They are particularly useful for scoring data gathered through observations, structured interviews, open-ended questions, student reports and self-inventories, and portfolios.

Analytic Scoring

Analytic scoring is a method that may be used to score students' use of metacognitive knowledge and skills over the course of a problem-solving exercise. They are also appropriate for diagnosing misconceptions or faulty knowledge structures about mathematical phenomena. For example, in scoring problem-solving performance, phases of the problem-solving enterprise are first identified and for each phase a scale is used to assign points. Teachers can assign points depending on whether students demonstrate metacognitive knowledge and skills in terms of understanding the nature of the problem, whether they are able to sift relevant from irrelevant information in a problem, whether they are able to select an appropriate strategy for problem solving or to select a form for representing information in the problem. Points may also be assigned should students obtain the correct answer. The same procedure may be used for judging the quantity and quality of the student's mathematical knowledge of concepts and principles as well as his or her knowledge structures underlying the mathematical problem of interest. These techniques are particularly suited for focused identification of relative strengths and weaknesses in specific factors underlying problem-solving performance. Teachers may use these for written and computer-assisted assessment data.

General Impression Scoring

General impression scoring produces one single number on a student's written problem-solving performance. Unlike analytic scoring, the teacher uses implicit criteria for rating the overall quality of students' problem-solving solutions. It is an efficient method for scoring short assignments and quizzes, but it is recommended only for teachers who have had extensive experience in analyzing students' problem-solving performance.

Summary

In this author's judgment, educationally at risk learners are products of our educational, social, and economic system. Their less than adequate performance on standardized tests combined with negative attitudes toward school experiences and low educational aspirations provided educators with the justification for labeling them "educationally at risk." Demographic, economic, and moral imperatives urge all those connected with the educational enterprise to provide nurturing experiences to improve their academic achievement in general and mathematical performance in particular. In 1989, the National Council of Teachers of Mathematics set forth lofty and ambitious standards for all children, including the educationally at risk learner. This is an encouraging sign and the council ought to be commended for embarking on such a bold and challenging initiative.

However, the problem of the educationally at risk learner is complex and multifaceted and standards, though important, are but the first step in the direction toward addressing the problem. In this chapter, the author has called attention to the importance of understanding the academic needs of the educationally at risk learner in terms of strengths and weaknesses underlying mathematics performance. A review of the research literature was conducted to determine the critical correlates underlying mathematical performance. It was revealed that underlying competencies included metacognitive knowledge and skills, a well-construed mathematical knowledge, and rich and well-organized knowledge structures. Further, the evidence suggested that the sociocultural context played a socializing role in influencing the quality of these competencies. The author presented a conceptualization of competence in mathematics and explored the implications of these under-standings for new assessment practices and suggested recom-mendations for educational policymakers and the classroom teacher. In conclusion, the problem of the educationally at risk learner is serious but not insurmountable. Whether we suc-ceed or not will depend not so much on our knowledge and understanding of the problem but rather upon our commitment and will to *act* upon that which we know and understand.

References

Anderson, R. (1984). "Some Reflections on the Acquisition of Knowledge." *Educational Researcher* 13: 5-10.

Artzt, A. F., and Armour-Thomas, E. (In Press). *Cognition and Instruction.*

Baker, E. L. (1991). "Developing Comprehensive Assessments of Higher Order Thinking." In G. Kulm, ed., *Assessing Higher Order Thinking in Mathematics.* American Association for the Advancement of Science, Washington, DC.

Branford, J. D., Sherwood, R. D., Kinzer, C. K., and Hasselbring, T. S. (1985). "Havens for Learning: Toward a Framework for Developing Effective Use of Technology" (Tech. Rep. No. 85.1.1). Nashville, TN: Learning Technology Center, Vanderbilt University.

Brown, A. L. (1978). Knowing When, Where, and How to Remember: A Problem of Metacognition." In R. Glaser, ed., *Advances in Instructional Psychology* (Vol. 1, 77-165). Hillsdale, NJ: Lawrence Erlbaum Associates.

Brown, J. S., and Burton, R. R. (1978). "Diagnostic Models for Procedural Bugs in Basic Mathematics." *Cognitive Science* 4: 379-426.

Carpenter, T. P. (1985). "Learning to Add and Subtract: An Exercise in Problem Solving." In E. A. Silver, ed., *Teaching and Learning Mathematical Problem Solving* . Hillsdale, NJ: Erlbaum.

Ceci, S. J. (1990). *On Intelligence. . .More or Less: A Bio-ecological Treatise on Intellectual Development.* Englewood Cliffs, NJ: Prentice Hall.

Coleman, J. S., Campbell, E. Q., Hobson, C. J., McPartland, J., Mood, A. A., Weinfeld, F. S., and York, R. L. (1966). *Equality of Educational Opportunity* (Report from the Office of Education). Washington, DC: U.S. Government Printing Office.

D' Ambrosio, U. (1985). *Da realidadeaacao: Reflexores sobre educacao e matematica.* Sao Paulo, Brazil: Summus Editorial.

Davis, R., and McKnight, C. (1980). "The Influence of Semantic Content on Algorithmic Behavior." *Journal of Mathematical Behavior* 3: 39-87.

Durken, J. H. (1981). *Secondary School Dropouts.* St. Paul, MN: Minnesota State Department of Education. (ERIC Document Reproduction Service No. ED 205 684.)

Ekstrom, R. E., Goertz, M. E., Pollack, J. M., and Rock, D. A. (1986). "Who Drops Out of School and Why: Findings from a National Study." *Teachers College Record* 87: 356-73.

Flavell, J. H. (1979). "Metacognition and Cognitive Monitoring: A New Area of Cognitive-Developmental Inquiry." *American Psychologist,* 34: 906-11.

Gagne, E., and Dick, W. (1983). "Instructional Psychology." In M. Rosenzweig and L. Porter, eds., *Annual Review of Psychology.* Palo Alto, CA: Annual Reviews.

Garofalo, J., and Lester, F. K. (1985). "Metacognition, Cognitive Monitoring, and Mathematical Performance." *Journal for Research in Mathematics Education* 16 (3): 163-76.

Geertz, C (1962). "The Growth of Culture and the Evolution of the Mind." In J. M. Scher, ed., *Theories of the Mind.* New York: Free Press.

Gelman, R., and Gallistel, C. R. (1978). *The Child's Understanding of Number.* Cambridge, MA: Harvard University Press.

Ghantala, E. S. (1986). "Strategy-Monitoring Training Enables Young Learners to Select Effective Strategies." *Educational Psychologist* 21: 43-54.

Glaser, R. (1987). "The Integration of Instruction and Testing: Implications from the Study of Human Cognition." In D. C. Berliner and B. V. Rosenshine, eds., *Talk to Teachers*. New York: Random House.

Gick, M. L., and Holyoak, K. J. (1980). "Analogical Problem Solving." *Cognitive Psychology* 12: 306-55.

Greeno, J. G., Riley, M. S., and Gelman, R. (1984). "Conceptual Competence and Children's Counting." *Cognitive Psychology* 16: 94-143.

Kagan, D. (1990). "How Schools Alienate Students at Risk: A Model for Examining Proximal Classroom Variables." *Educational Psychologist* 25 (2): 105-25.

Lave, J., Murtaugh, M., and de la Roche, O. (1984). "The Dialectic of Arithmetic in Grocery Shopping." In B. Rogoff and J. Lave, eds., *Everyday Cognition: Its Development in Social Context*. Cambridge, MA: Harvard University Press.

Martz, M. (1980). "Toward a Computational Model of Algebraic Competence. *Journal of Mathematical Behavior* 3: 93-166.

National Council of Teachers of Mathematics (1989). *Curriculum and Evaluation Standards for School Mathematics*. Reston, VA: The Council.

Oakes, J. (1990). *Multiplying Inequities. The Effects of Race, Socioeconomic Status and Tracking on Opportunities to Learn Mathematics and Science*. Santa Monica, CA: The Rand Corporation.

Pallas, A. M., Natriello, G., and McDill, E. L. (1989). "The Changing Nature of the Disadvantaged Population: Current Dimensions and Future Trends." *Educational Researcher* 18 (5): 16-22.

Peng, S. S., and Takai, R. T. (1983). *High School Dropouts: Descriptive Information from High School and Beyond.* Washington, DC: National Center for Educational Statistics. (ERIC Document Reproduction Service No. ED 236 366.)

Peterson, P. L. (1988). "Teachers and Students' Cognitional Knowledge for Classroom Teaching and Learning." *Educational Researcher* 17 (5): 5-14.

Peterson, P.L., and Swing, S. R., Braverman, M. T., & Buss, R. (1982). "Students' Aptitudes and Their Reports of Cognitive Processes during Direct Instruction." *Journal of Educational Psychology,* 74 (4): 535-47.

Peterson, P. L., Swing, S. R., Stark, K. D., and Waas, G. A. (1984). "Students' Cognitions and Time on Task During Mathematics Instruction." *American Educational Research Journal,* 21: 487-515.

Resnick, L. B. (1987). *Education and Learning to Think.* Washington, DC: National Academy Press.

---. (1984). "Beyond Error Analysis: The Role of Understanding in Elementary School Arithmetic." In H. Cheek, eds., *Diagnostic and Prescriptive Mathematics: Issues Ideas and Insight.* Hillsdale, NJ: Erlbaum. 1992.

---. (1982). "Syntax and Semantics in Learning to Subtract." In T. Carpenter, J. Moser, and T. Romberg, eds., *Addition and Subtraction: A Cognitive Perspective.* New York: Academic Press.

Rumberger, R. W. (1987). "High School Dropouts: A Review of Issues and Evidence." *Review of Educational Research* 57: 101-21.

Saxe, G. B. (1988). "Candy Selling and Math Learning." *Educational Researcher.* 17 (6): 14-21.

Schreiber, D. (1979). "Dropout--Causes and Consequences." In R. L. Ebel, ed., *Encyclopedia of Educational Research* (4th ed.). Toronto: Macmillan.

Scribner, S. (1984). "Studying Working Intelligence." In B. Rogoff and J. Lave, eds., *Everyday Cognition: Its Development in Social Context*. Cambridge, MA: Harvard University Press.

Silver, E. A. (1987). "Foundations of Cognitive Theory and Research for Mathematics Problem Solving Instruction." In A. H. Schoenfeld, ed., *Cognitive Science and Mathematics Education*. Hillsdale, NJ: Lawrence Erlbaum Associates.

Shoenfeld, A. H. (1987). "What's All the Fuss about Metacognition?" In A. H. Schoenfeld, ed., *Cognitive Science and Mathematics Education*. Hillsdale, NJ: Erlbaum.

Sternberg, R. J. (1986). *Intelligence Applied*. San Diego, CA: Harcourt Brace Jovanovich.

Whitehead, A. N. (1929). *The Aims of Education*. New York: MacMillan

Zuboff, S. (1988). *In the Age of the Smart Machine: The Future of Work and Power*. New York: Basic Books.

DO YOU HAVE AN IDEA TO SHARE?

The National Educational Service is always looking for high-quality manuscripts that have practical application for educators and others who work with youth.

Do you have a new, innovative, or especially effective approach to some timely issue? Does one of your colleagues have something burning to say on curriculum development, professionalism in education, excellence in teaching, or some other aspect of education? If so, let us know. We would like to hear from you. Tell us that reading *Nurturing At-Risk Youth in Math and Science* gave you an incentive to contact us.

Nancy Shin, Director of Publications
National Educational Service
1610 West Third Street
P.O. Box 8
Bloomington, IN 47402
1-800-733-6786
or
1-812-336-7700

NEED MORE COPIES?

Need more copies of this book? Want your own copy? If so, you can order additional copies of *Nurturing At-Risk Youth in Math and Science: Curriculum and Teaching Considerations* by using this form or by calling us at (800) 733-6786 (US only) or (812) 336-7700. Or you can order by FAX at (812) 336-7790.

We guarantee complete satisfaction with all of our materials. If you are not completely satisfied with any NES publication, you may return it to us within 30 days for a full refund.

	Quantity	**Total**
Nurturing At-Risk Youth in Math and Science: Curriculum and Teaching Considerations ($19.95 each)	_____	_____
Shipping: Add $2.00 per copy		_____
(There is no shipping charge when you *include* payment with your order)		
Indiana residents add 5% sales tax		_____
TOTAL		_____

❏ Check enclosed with order   ❏ Please bill me

❏ VISA or MasterCard   ❏ Money order

❏ P.O.#_____

Account No._____ Exp. Date _____

Cardholder _____

Ship to:

Name_____Title _____

Organization _____

Address _____

City_____State_____ ZIP _____

Phone _____

MAIL TO:
National Educational Service
1610 W. Third Street
P.O. Box 8
Bloomington, IN 47402

Nurturing At-Risk Youth in Math and Science: Curriculum and Teaching Considerations is one of the many publications produced by the National Educational Service. Our mission is to provide you and other leaders in education, business, and government with timely, top-quality publications, videos, and conferences. If you have any questions or comments about *Nurturing At-Risk Youth in Math and Science* or if you want information on in-service training or professional development on any of the following topics:

Discipline with Dignity
Reclaiming Youth at Risk
Cooperative Learning
Thinking Across the Curriculum
Cooperative Management
Parental Involvement

Contact us at:

National Educational Service
1610 West Third Street
P.O. Box 8
Bloomington, IN 47402